Michael Ange
Barnard, and

WIREFRAMING FOR EVERYONE

MORE FROM A BOOK APART

Immersive Content and Usability
Preston So

The Business of UX Writing
Yael Ben-David

Inclusive Design Communities
Sameera Kapila

Leading Content Design
Rachel McConnell

You Should Write a Book
Katel LeDû and Lisa Maria Marquis

Responsible JavaScript
Jeremy Wagner

SEO for Everyone
Rebekah Baggs and Chris Corak

Design for Safety
Eva PenzeyMoog

Voice Content and Usability
Preston So

Better Onboarding
Krystal Higgins

Visit abookapart.com for our full list of titles.

Publisher: Jeffrey Zeldman
Designer: Jason Santa Maria
Executive director: Katel LeDû
Editor in chief: Lisa Maria Marquis
Editors: Sharina Wunderink, Susan Bond, Jen Mediano
Book producer: Ron Bilodeau
Illustrations: Laura Lei

ISBN: 978-1-952616-22-8

A Book Apart
New York, New York
http://abookapart.com

10 9 8 7 6 5 4 3 2 1

TABLE OF CONTENTS

*To anyone dreaming of turning ideas into products, you got this.
For Ali, Lorenzo, and Kai, who champion my creativity and inspire
me every day—all my love.*

—Michael

*To all the live wireframing session participants I met
who are doing important and meaningful work without a
designer, this book is for you.*

—Leon

*To the countless folks I've met as an educator, who are working
hard to develop careers in design. It's a difficult but worthwhile
challenge. Don't give up. To Michelle, Will, Annie, Coco, and
Gigi, who make each day an adventure.*

—Billy

FOREWORD

I'VE USED WIREFRAMES throughout my entire career. Wire-frames helped me learn how to understand and talk about design principles in college. They were instrumental in landing my dream job at Kickstarter. They've always been an integral part of my day-to-day work as a product manager, leader, and founder.

There's a reason why wireframing continues to be a key practice in my work.

Wireframing is such a powerful tool because it's both collaborative and accessible. Unlike skills that take years to develop, or software that takes extensive training to use, wireframing can benefit you on your very first try. It's a tool that gets your product ideas out of your head and onto the page or screen—where everyone on your team can work on them together. But few of us have been explicitly taught how to wireframe, and this is where Wireframing for Everyone comes in.

If you haven't created your own wireframes before, this book will not only help you get started—it'll get you hooked. It gives you permission, vocabulary, and tools to move from abstract ideas to concrete designs, even if you've never thought of yourself as a designer before. You could draw your first wireframe today to visualize a product concept. Tomorrow, that same wireframe might help you answer a new question about features. Next week, it could explain design requirements to your coworker. Wireframes are tools for thinking, communicating, and engaging your colleagues throughout the entire design process.

Whether you're experienced with or newly curious about wireframing, this book will inspire you to go from blank canvas, to collaborative discussion, to shaping final product design with confidence. Michael, Leon, and Billy guide you through using essential techniques, getting comfortable with a shared vocabulary, and integrating wireframes into your workflow—starting today.

—Ellen Chisa

WHY WIREFRAMES (STILL) MATTER

THERE ARE FEW RESOURCES that effectively explain user interface (UI) design in a real working environment. You'll often see tools and techniques described in ideal scenarios, but you'll rarely find discussions about how to deliver a great design experience among overflowing backlogs, tight deadlines, and demands for must-have features. To make better decisions and produce more effective products, we need to understand not only how design tools and techniques work, but also how they can build better relationships across our teams.

That's what this book about wireframing is for.

Wireframes are an effective tool for designing user interfaces, and, because of their simplicity, an effective way to learn the craft of UI design. Wireframing is a language for communicating user interface ideas, which helps developers, designers, product managers, and stakeholders think about and understand the big-picture structure of a website or app without being distracted by the details.

Despite the rapid growth of user experience (UX) as a profession, that communication is still necessary. Many organizations aren't fully invested in UX or don't know how to integrate it into their existing process. This creates a gap for teams who *want* to design better but don't have the resources or leadership they need to get there.

However, having powerful UX tools and a talented designer on your team won't magically yield a great experience for your end user. Great experiences emerge from teams where *everyone* can participate in the design process. We've witnessed the power of informal, low-fidelity design that invites the whole team into the design process.

Among design artifacts, wireframes are unique in that anyone can create and understand them. They function as a tool for both ideation and practical communication. Empowered with an understanding of how designers think and some basic user interface design literacy—both of which we teach in this book—you'll have everything you need to build wireframes to support amazing products.

There are many reasons to explore wireframing and many ways using wireframes can help your product and your team. Whatever path led you to pick up this book, you're in the right place if you want to design better software and collaborate more effectively.

THE ENDURING POWER OF LOW FIDELITY

A usability researcher we know told us a story that echoes experiences we've observed in modern software organizations. After six months spent designing and building a web app, the project lead put a testable version of the product in front of users—and watched each user struggle with it.

The design, while content rich and polished, missed key elements that users expected. The design team went from specifications directly to creating polished visual designs and prototypes. When the internal reviewers signed off, based on branding and feasibility, the developers were ready to start coding.

Everyone involved learned a painful lesson about moving in a singular design direction that had focused on creating a finished-looking prototype. The existing work had to be scrapped, costing time and money. Had the team explored and evaluated

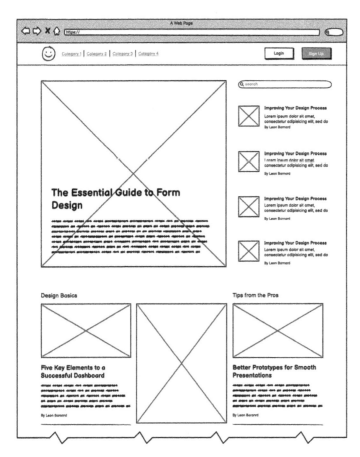

FIG 1.1: A wireframe shows the elements of a product design but with minimal styling, giving your team a distraction-free visual reference for exploring ideas relating to the product's function and content.

multiple design ideas along the way using wireframes, they likely would have found a more usable solution.

So, what is a *wireframe*, exactly, and what purpose does it serve? A wireframe is a rough schematic created in the early stages of digital product design to help you and your team think and communicate about the structure of a product or website (**FIG 1.1**).

As product designers and educators, we regularly observe and assess how teams use wireframes to build products. We've seen and heard countless examples of how wireframing has helped teams explore design concepts and—more importantly—discuss, test, and improve their ideas until the best solution emerged. Wireframes serve as an objective tool to align teams and stakeholders, and to keep projects moving forward.

We use wireframes to both illustrate and articulate what a product will do. They're created using a hybrid of *sketching* (a technique for capturing rough ideas quickly) and *prototyping* (a technique for demonstrating functionality that more closely resembles a final product). By harnessing the most effective aspects of each technique, wireframes tend to provide more information than sketches alone, and the process of creating them encourages more exploration than prototyping alone.

The primary benefit of wireframes to software organizations isn't their ability to represent a user interface but their ability to visualize and facilitate the transformation from idea to code—in the same way that a napkin sketch can instantly cause one person to understand what another is talking about. The *understanding* is the output.

That's why it's helpful to think of wireframes as more like sketches than prototypes. In a wireframe, like a sketch, you leave things out on purpose in order to focus on the idea. The lack of *fidelity*—and the ability to stand in for the real thing—works in its favor.

Starting out at a very low level of granularity allows you to evolve the design deliberately by moving on to finer levels of detail only as you become more confident about the coarser ones (**FIG 1.2**). One of the mottos of wireframing is: "fidelity should correspond to certainty."

This isn't only apparent in digital design. Low-fidelity ideation is the foundation for creative work in architecture, painting, sculpture, performance art, automobile design, animation, and film.

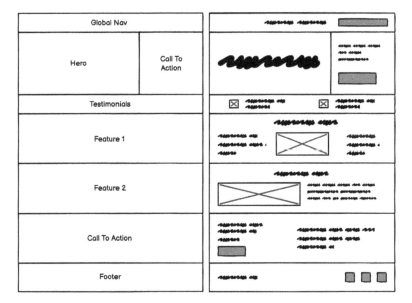

FIG 1.2: Great wireframes start out at low levels of fidelity (realism) and increase incrementally to allow the most important decisions and discussions to happen first.

Elizabeth Francis, the architect who designed the Balsamiq offices, shared an example of how she typically sketches out an early floor plan concept to imagine possible configurations of an interior space (**FIG 1.3**).

Even with access to dedicated architectural software, Francis prefers to create early sketches by hand to share with her clients. In his book *Sketching User Experiences*, Bill Buxton says that sketches are characterized by "the freedom, energy, abandon, and looseness of the lines" (https://bkaprt.com/wfe45/01-01, PDF). The result, he says, is that a sketch "does not represent a refined proposal, but rather simply suggests a tentative concept."

If you've ever wondered why digital wireframes often have a hand-drawn effect applied, this is why. Amid all the uncertainty in a complex software project, showing user interface designs that approximate a final product can give viewers a false sense of confidence in their readiness.

FIG 1.3: In architecture, low-fidelity sketches are used early in the design process. Photograph courtesy of Atelier Francis.

WIREFRAMES THROUGHOUT THE DESIGN PROCESS

We've learned from numerous teams who have given us insights about how they've used wireframes to launch successful products—and they share a strong, common theme: they use a structured, repeatable process.

Many popular design processes encourage separate phases of divergence and convergence to arrive at the best solution. *Divergent thinking* is at the heart of creativity and centers around creating as many ideas as possible without restriction. *Convergent thinking* is the opposite and encourages you to inspect and reject ideas to reduce the number of successful possibilities.

Wireframing uniquely supports both divergent and convergent processes. That is, wireframes are both easy to make *and* easy to change. This is different from, for example, pencil and paper sketches, which are easy to make, but difficult to change, and prototypes, which can take time to create and are often arduous to revise.

The key to using wireframes throughout the design process is to adapt them for each phase. During the course of design, the number of wireframes expands as you create and explore ideas, and then narrows as you review and refine. (**FIG 1.4**).

But it's not only the volume of wireframes that changes over time—the level of fidelity also changes at different design phases. Early low- and medium-fidelity outputs require minimal time and effort to make, and allow just the right amount of detail to emerge during idea exploration. Later-phase wireframes help bring in more perspectives and push ideas toward execution.

Early-phase wireframes

When you first start wireframing, your goals should be to:

1. Get your ideas out of your head and onto the screen or page, and
2. Use what comes out to generate new ideas.

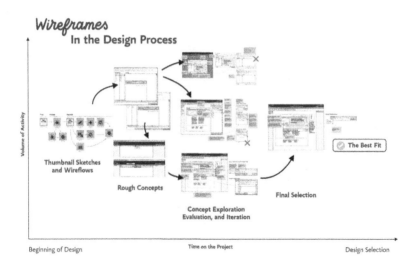

Wireframes
In the Design Process

Volume of Activity

Thumbnail Sketches
and Wireflows

Rough Concepts

Concept Exploration
Evaluation, and Iteration

Final Selection

The Best Fit

Beginning of Design | Time on the Project | Design Selection

FIG 1.4: The wireframing process should result in many variations and types of wireframes before you land on the best fit.

In this phase it's common to use pencil and paper, although digital tools work too. The key is to move quickly, so do whatever works best for you.

Early-phase, ultra-low-fidelity wireframes should be purposefully rough in appearance, whether made by hand or digitally. They're typically drawn with imprecise lines and use a single color. They may be abstract, and short on content and design details.

Over the years, we've discovered many people have preconceptions about designing interfaces that prevent them from making the most of wireframing. Unlike a prototype, which must accurately reflect the final product, we determine a wireframe's effectiveness by the conversations it creates. Letting go of unconscious rules about what a design artifact should look like can lead to better early-phase wireframes.

In this phase, wireframes (sketches, really) can be low fidelity (**FIG 1.5-6**) or even "no fidelity"—drawings like flow charts, content models, or other diagrams (**FIG 1.7-8**). Both low- and no-fidelity wireframes usually consist of basic shapes, arrows, and text, rather than specific user interface elements. If you find

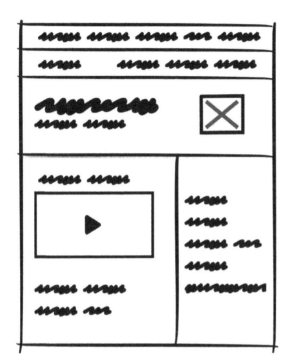

FIG 1.5: A low-fidelity sketch with very little detail.

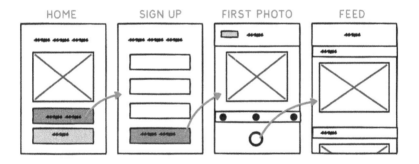

FIG 1.6: Early-phase wireframes shouldn't be any more detailed than this.

yourself adding more detail in the beginning than what we've described, step back and make sure you're not spending too much time on any one idea.

FIG 1.7: Early wireframes often start out by simply defining placeholders for the content.

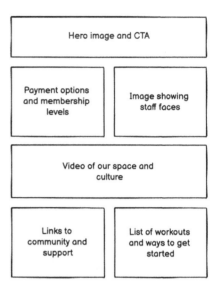

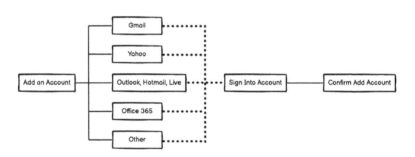

FIG 1.8: When starting out, it's common to begin simply with a diagram of user options or screen connections.

The more ideas you start with, the better. And when those ideas aren't fully fleshed out, then they're likely to inspire more ideas. In *Sketching User Interfaces,* Bill Buxton suggests focusing less on the artifacts created in this phase and more on the process of sketching, calling the sketches themselves "the vehicle, not the destination." He concludes with the koan, "There is much more to the activity of sketching than making sketches."

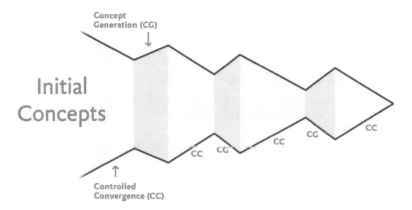

FIG 1.9: In practice, convergence is more effective when you allow yourself phases of divergence to explore variations (based on a concept by Stuart Pugh).

Middle-phase wireframes

Once you've sown the seeds of your initial ideas, you can shift your thinking toward making sense of them—but not completely. It's too simplistic to think of this phase as two lines converging smoothly toward one ideal solution, where the winners move on and the losers are left behind. Instead, the mantra for this phase could be "combine and refine," where you cultivate and improve upon the good ideas.

One of the mistakes people make while wireframing is to pick the favorite idea from the previous phase and move ahead with it. But one of the biggest challenges (and rewards) of wireframing is to linger in uncertainty. After your first round of wireframing, there's still so much that you don't know.

In *Total Design: Integrated Methods for Successful Product Engineering*, Stuart Pugh visualizes convergence as a series of alternating smaller steps of convergence and divergence (which he calls "controlled convergence" and "concept generation," respectively) that decrease, then briefly increase, the number of ideas, before converging again and again (**FIG 1.9**).

The takeaway is that you should allow new ideas to emerge as you evaluate existing ones. Be willing to let go of weaker ideas to make space for stronger ones. Not getting too attached

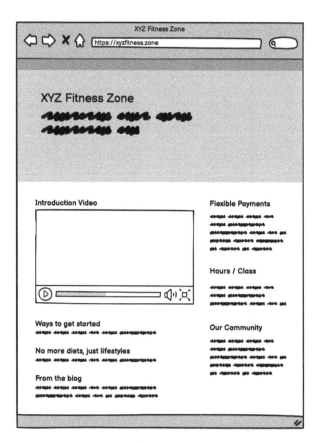

FIG 1.10: Middle-phase wireframes might introduce some real text as well as UI elements.

to any one idea will make it easier to generate and evaluate concepts, eliminate the ones that don't work, and focus on improving the ones that do.

Middle-phase wireframes are a step above sketches when it comes to fidelity (**FIG 1.10**). To be most effective, however, treat them like sketches—impermanent and draft like. Use a limited color palette to avoid getting overly detailed. Like sketches, the fidelity of these wireframes is less important than the ideas you're trying to communicate.

This is also the phase when you can begin the transition from idea to product, and start thinking about how users will interact with each screen and navigate among them. You may experiment with different layouts or components for the same basic workflows. The variations and changes can become more granular here. We will explore techniques for this in Chapter 3.

Later-phase wireframes

Your goal in later phases of the design process is to improve the way your wireframes communicate ideas and invite discussion. In this phase, successful wireframing requires being comfortable with softening the separation between external and internal audiences. It's fine to show screens or pages designed for end users alongside annotations and text meant for developers and other stakeholders.

Just because you're later in the process doesn't mean your wireframes should be high fidelity. High-fidelity wireframes look real enough to be confused with an actual product and may include interactive behavior, so they're really prototypes at that point. If your project lead or client requests "high fidelity," you're usually better off creating a *comp* (short for comprehensive) or *mockup* that looks indistinguishable from a real product.

Rather than thinking about making later-phase wireframes more realistic, instead start thinking about how to optimize them for a different audience: your colleagues and stakeholders. Once you've clarified and pruned your wireframes during the first two phases, the next step will be to share them, which includes making them easy to understand and follow. You can do this by adding more detail, at critical or novel interactions, by showing real or sample content, including annotations, and by paying more attention to the flow between and within screens (**FIG 1.11-12**).

By the time you reach this stage with your wireframes, you'll have spent so much time with them that you might find it easy to become attached to them. In this phase, your biggest danger is getting too invested in your wireframes. Try to resist! People

HOME SCREEN   SIGN UP

FIG 1.11: Later-phase wireframes should be able to stand on their own without needing a designer to explain them.

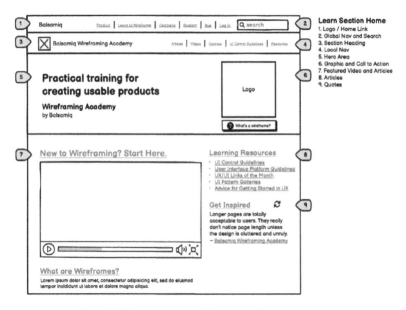

FIG 1.12: Later-phase wireframes use more real content and annotations.

with specialized knowledge of the domain users or technology will have to judge, critique, test, and validate your wireframes. This is the final stage of their journey.

WHAT MAKES A WIREFRAME GOOD?

Wireframing is the first step toward making more successful products, but making the most of your wireframes is the bigger challenge. The hardest question we asked ourselves when planning this book was, "What makes a wireframe *good?*"

It depends, of course, but not in the way that you might expect. Unlike a digital prototype, we don't judge a wireframe by how much it looks like the final product. Rather, good wireframes pave the way to good products by bringing out the best ideas and shepherding them to implementation when we use the following techniques.

Embrace iteration

Good wireframes are the product of many rounds of iteration. Take advantage of the ease with which you can quickly create and change a lot of ideas. With their rough and disposable feel, wireframes encourage you to start over when you've hit a dead end. Because the truth, is that *many* of our ideas aren't winners. The most successful products result from taking risks. You have to be okay with being wrong many times in order to get the design right.

Successful iterative design depends on your willingness to regard ideas as ephemeral so that you can let go of weaker ideas in favor of finding the best ones. The best ideas are the ones that provide the most effective solutions.

Ed Catmull, cofounder of Pixar and coauthor of *Creativity, Inc*, wrote about the importance of iteration and failure (https://bkaprt.com/wfe45/01-02). He called failure a "manifestation of learning and exploration." The process of making an animated film at Pixar involves producing *reels*—videos using storyboard images stitched together with placeholder music and voices—to visualize and get feedback on the story script before ever moving on to animation. A single ninety-minute reel requires about twelve thousand storyboard drawings, and up to ten reels are created per film—meaning the creative team makes up to *120,000* drawings by the time their work is done! This proves that however great the first idea may feel, it very likely won't end up in the final product. In truth, expecting to ship your first idea is probably a red flag.

Coincidentally—or perhaps not—René Redzepi, co-owner of the three-Michelin-star restaurant Noma, has said that for every amazing idea that comes out, you need ten ideas to come in (https://bkaprt.com/wfe45/01-03). The best solutions never start as perfect, fully formed ideas.

Identify and bridge the gaps

Our earlier story about the unfortunate usability researcher would've turned out differently if the team had explored even a few ideas at lower fidelity. If they'd tested and evaluated multiple concepts along the way, they could have seen where they'd veered off course and could have steered in a better direction.

An important goal to have when you start wireframing is to let the wireframes help you see what's missing. First, you want to transfer the ideas you have in your head onto the screen or page. This will show you gaps or flaws in your ideas once you see them in front of you. Sketching out the flow should show you areas or use cases you forgot to think through. The image in your head is always fuzzier than you think it is.

Your first wireframes and the reactions they generate should encourage exploration. Seeing what's missing will lead you to think of more and better ideas. A good wireframe's open-endedness should prompt ideation—the spark that ignites creativity—and iteration.

Solve the right problem

A good wireframe should be designed from the user's point-of-view and present solutions that work for its intended user.

In her book, *Designing Interfaces*, Jenifer Tidwell wrote, "The real art of interface design lies *in solving the right problem*" (https://bkaprt.com/wfe45/01-04). A great design solution for a poorly defined problem is infinitely worse than a decent solution applied to a well-defined problem.

Good wireframes show that you understand your audience, their goals, and a real problem that they have. We recommend that you write this information down in your wireframes. This can feel tedious, but it's the *most important* part of the entire process. It will have the biggest impact on the end product.

If you have user research artifacts such as personas, journey maps, or usage data, they will come in handy. But even if you don't, you need to articulate a few basic details about the problem and document them in a central, accessible place for everyone involved in your project.

You're only really ready to wireframe once you've answered three essential questions:

1. **Who will use the design solution?** Try to capture the intended audience(s) using clear, unambiguous terminology that everyone can understand. If you have personas, refer to them. If not, refer to known role types, such as "admins" or "donors."
2. **What are the user's goals?** Establish success criteria for users. Frame goals around user needs, not yours. For example, users don't want to sign up for a service, but they may want some of the benefits of signing up, such as being able to save their progress and come back later to continue.
3. **What problem(s) does this design address?** State the concerns users have with your existing product, problems they have with competitors' products, or other frustrations they encounter that your product addresses.

This is a short list, but it's important to write it out so that you can see it as you design. If you're using a wireframing tool, you can use the notes area, or a sticky note on the first page, to write down who your users are, what their goals are, and what problems they have (**FIG 1.13**).

Documenting user needs helps the team align around this critical information. It also puts you into the problem-solving mindset required for wireframing, so you'll approach it more like a whiteboard rather than a tool for creating an attractive interface.

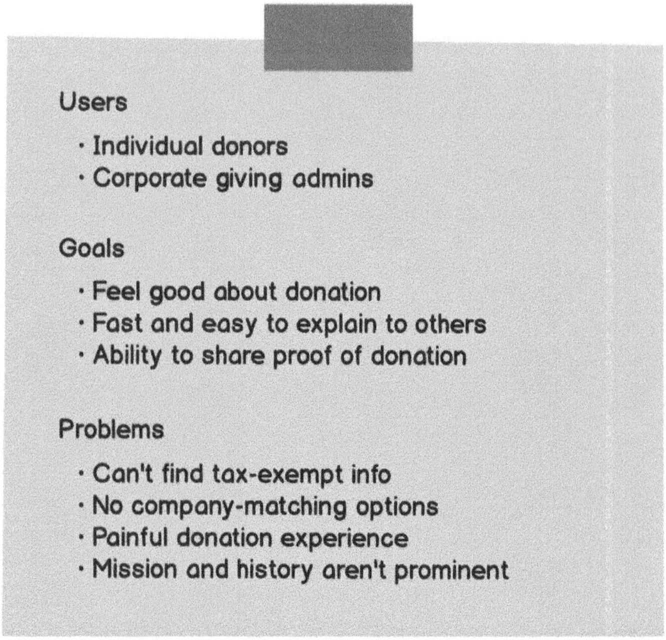

Users

- Individual donors
- Corporate giving admins

Goals

- Feel good about donation
- Fast and easy to explain to others
- Ability to share proof of donation

Problems

- Can't find tax-exempt info
- No company-matching options
- Painful donation experience
- Mission and history aren't prominent

FIG 1.13: Placing a note on the first page of your wireframe project—describing the users, their goals, and their problems—will help keep your designs focused on the users.

Invite action

Wireframes have two audiences: you, and your collaborators. Good wireframes don't only help you visualize your ideas in the beginning; they help you communicate them once they come into focus. When you're ready to show your wireframes to others, the goal changes. Now, it's a blueprint for a real product.

Good wireframes invite discussion. Adding annotations such as notes or comments can help. You can further achieve this by making sure that your wireframe isn't overly polished or final, and by even leaving areas unfinished on purpose.

As we mentioned earlier, you should also be able to understand later-phase wireframes on their own. This means adding descriptions, adding arrows to connect pages, and including all screens or steps in the workflow. Think about how you can add a layer of context to increase clarity.

The most challenging part of creating a good later-phase wireframe is including the right amount of detail. If you don't provide enough, then it won't be able to stand on its own, but if you include too much, then it isn't open-ended enough for further iteration. There's no firm guide, but pay attention to when you begin to encounter diminishing returns on the information the audience needs to know relative to the effort it takes to convey it.

The result should produce a clear idea of the proposed options and what you need to do next. This could mean highlighting the differences between what currently exists and what a design puts forward, or highlighting the areas of least certainty. The reaction you *don't* want from others is, "Ok, now what?" A good wireframe allows the next person to pick it up and run with it.

WIREFRAMING TOOLS

Wireframing has gotten a bad rap for a while now. The software development industry is flush with tools that allow nearly anyone to create realistic user interfaces that scale responsively, animate and scroll, and let anyone with a web browser interact with them. Compared with the outputs of modern prototyping tools, wireframes feel primitive.

On the other end of the spectrum, the market for sketching and drawing by hand is booming. There are websites dedicated to the best notebooks and pens, describing their weight, texture, and materials in detail. Highly sensitive touchscreens and precise styli exist for digital artists and thinkers. Digital whiteboards capture ideation and planning sessions. Paper and pencil, the most primitive tool of all, evokes infinite possibilities.

This is the trap that technology creates. A tool or a product that does more isn't necessarily a better one. Limitations and constraints, as we'll show, can lead to more creative and appropriate solutions.

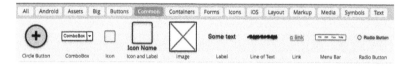

FIG 1.14: A useful feature of a dedicated wireframing tool is a comprehensive library of UI components that you can mix and match to quickly create interface concepts.

You can wireframe using whatever method or tool feels right to you. Some people get so energized by the feel of pen on paper that it's worth the extra effort to start over for every new or different idea. Others live in their prototyping or visual design tools and can't imagine using anything else. We get it.

The most important feature in a wireframing tool is that it helps you visualize new ideas as fast as they come to you. It should not interrupt your flow. This is why pen and paper or marker and whiteboards are popular for wireframing, especially in the early stages of design when you're trying to generate multiple divergent ideas.

If you want to use software, here are two things we find helpful in choosing a tool:

1. The software should contain a library of user interface component types that you can quickly add to the screen, especially for middle- and later-phase wireframing. This will help you move past basic shapes to components that can be written in code (**FIG 1.14**).

2. Software should not provide options for fine-tuning the elements of each component. Unless you are very disciplined, it's easy to get distracted by precise pixel dimensions, CSS properties, and interactive behavior. You don't need these options in order to wireframe.

TRUST THE PROCESS

Wireframing is a proven method for creating successful products because it identifies flaws early on, invites discussion, and lets the best ideas emerge before anybody starts writing code.

If you've ever been involved in a software project that has gone off the rails after coding starts, then you know both the pain of making changes later and the feeling that there must have been a way to know about the problems earlier. This is why wireframing matters. A thoughtful wireframing process can save you time and money, as well as pain and regret.

Anyone working on a software product can take advantage of wireframing to reduce anxiety about whether or not it's headed in the right direction. Wireframing helps teams to align while they work together to identify the problem and explore solutions. This collaborative effort builds trust and confidence in the team and the process.

2
EXPLORING IDEAS

" *You are a creator; do not be afraid to create.*
—**WILLIAM NTIM, 101 RANDOM UX TIPS** (https://bkaprt.com/wfe45/02-01)

WIREFRAMING IS A LOT LIKE WRITING. You start out with nothing but a spark of an idea and the vastness of a blank page—and the promise of winding up somewhere equally terrible or terrific.

It's no surprise that writers love to write about writing, and we can learn a lot from their habits. One great writing tip that applies to early-stage wireframes comes from Anne Lamott in *Bird by Bird*: "The first draft is the child's draft, where you let it all pour out and then let it romp all over the place."

In this chapter, we'll show you how to create the wireframe equivalent of a rough draft, or put another way, how to get an idea out of your head and onto the screen.

Writers often take two primary paths to producing a rough draft, depending on their content and writing style. The first is to *freewrite* or attempt to get every thought, idea fragment, and objective onto the page without attempting to organize, filter, or refine. The second path is to *outline*—using structure, organization, and high-level ideas—to create a skeleton upon which to build.

Wireframing uses the same techniques. Even if one path comes more naturally to you, both are effective, and the best wireframes come from some combination of both strategies.

CREATING STRUCTURE

Before you get too excited about creating your Pulitzer Prize-worthy wireframe, let's remember that what you're "writing" is more like a technical manual than the Great American Novel. Keep in mind that you're designing for real people. Your goal is to solve their problem in an effective and easy-to-understand way—not to immerse them in a story.

If you're working on a small project, you might find it most productive to start by freewriting: scribble your ideas on the page or screen as quickly as possible. But for medium to large projects involving multiple steps or screens, start with the writer's equivalent of an outline—just as someone writing a book might break up drafts into chapters, or even sketch out the entire story arc first.

Regardless of the type of product you're designing, you should spend some time sketching out the high-level path for your user to get to where they want to go. This can reduce the risk of losing sight of the connections between screens, which can happen if you design each step independently. In her article, "Documenting is designing: How documentation drives better design outcomes," designer Heidi Adkisson wrote, "One of the best ways to ensure a design is well-reasoned is to be 'forced' to describe it verbally or by flowing out the logic" (https://bkaprt.com/wfe45/02-02). Let's look at three artifacts that can help you create overarching structure for your wireframing project: sitemaps, user flows, and wireflows.

Sitemaps

Sitemaps are useful for thinking through a website hierarchy. They allow you to show high-level organization, and to con-

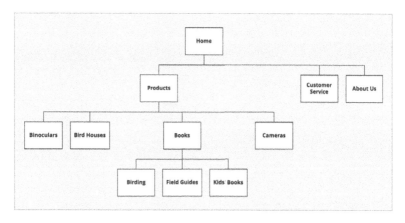

FIG 2.1: This sitemap for a hypothetical outdoor gear website shows navigation by category and sub-category.

sider how users might navigate around a site. In a sitemap, pages at nested levels in a hierarchy are shown as *parent-child* relationships and pages that are at parallel levels are shown as *sibling* relationships (**FIG 2.1**).

Sitemaps are best suited for sites or apps without too many pages or levels of hierarchy, but you can also truncate them at a certain level to make them more compact, since the first few levels of hierarchy are often the most useful. Knowing how many *child* objects a category has can be helpful when it comes to designing navigation—there are different solutions for four versus four thousand, for example.

In many cases you'll be working from an existing product, so you can start by creating a sitemap of what currently exists. This can help you see what might be confusing to users, areas where you can consolidate or separate categories, or even how you might group sub-pages in a completely different way.

Sitemaps are invaluable in the early phases of a project—they help visualize relationships and possible connections within your product. But keep in mind that a sitemap doesn't necessarily represent the way users will interact with, flow through, or conceptualize the site. In *Everyday Information Architecture*, Lisa Maria Marquis says, "sitemaps are not meant to capture

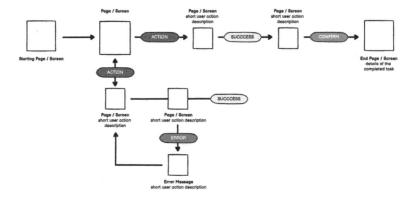

FIG 2.2: A user flow typically consists of boxes, arrows, and text describing the steps or screens needed to make every step visible. Without a user flow, you risk overlooking uncommon workflows, such as password recovery.

---

every possible path; indirect relationships between pages, and creative ways of surfacing content, won't necessarily appear here" (https://bkaprt.com/wfe45/02-03). So, don't wireframe your navigation solely based on your sitemap.

User flows

Rather than showing the structure of the *system*, a *user flow* presents the journey a user might take to complete a task. Visualizing this allows you to evaluate the task's complexity and think about how to simplify it. Importantly, user flows often reveal critical interactions you'll want to wireframe (**FIG 2.2**).

User flows are especially helpful when you have specific use cases or scenarios that you want or expect users to follow. This is common in applications (e.g., posting a photo to their feed) and ecommerce websites (e.g., adding a product to their cart) where there is a clear goal or destination. You can refer to the goals and problems list that you created earlier to identify use cases to focus on.

When creating a user flow, it can be helpful to start at the end because it keeps you focused on creating an optimal path. Label the end state with a box that represents the screen the user sees

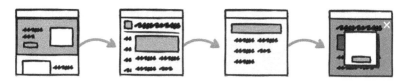

FIG 2.3: This wireflow adds high-level interface design details to a user flow diagram for a newsletter subscription project. We've created a wireflow library, available for download (https://bkaprt.com/wfe45/02-04).

when they have successfully completed their task, then work backward to how they got there until you reach the intended starting point (e.g., home page, search result, or clicking a link someone sent in an email).

Then take this ideal scenario (referred to as the *happy path* in UX jargon) to create a basic user flow and step through it from the beginning, this time thinking through what could go wrong along the way, or what other paths the user could take. Add these to your user flow as needed. You don't need to show or design every scenario, but be explicit about the flows that you do exclude so that you don't forget them.

Wireflows

Wireflows combine the features of wireframes and user flows to visualize both the user's path *and* basic elements of the interface design. They consist of a series of wireframes with arrows showing how they connect to each other (**FIG 2.3**).

The individual wireframes intentionally lack detail so that viewers can focus on the steps or actions users may perform to navigate between them. It's easier to refine or change the interface than to rethink the underlying connections critical to the foundation of the experience.

Wireflows allow you to start putting some of the UI pieces in place while staying focused on the user flow and optimizing it for the user. You don't need to include every interaction or choice the user makes; it's more useful to record how and when the interface changes, so you can focus on those screens when creating wireframes.

LAYING A FOUNDATION

Content is critical to wireframes, because without it, you don't actually know how much space to leave for it.
—LAURA KLEIN, UX FOR LEAN STARTUPS (https://bkaprt.com/wfe45/02-05/)

At the beginning of a design project, you might be tempted to jump right into translating the picture in your mind into the visual interface. It can be so gratifying to create form where there once wasn't!

Most people think of interface design as drawing boxes inside of other boxes, starting with the app or browser window and dividing it into increasingly smaller sections. But if you draw these boxes arbitrarily or without examination, they won't match their contents.

More worthwhile (and challenging) is to let form and structure emerge in relationship to the content. Give the content the form *it wants*, rather than forcing it into an ill-fitting structure.

When users visit websites, they seek information—what something costs, business hours of operation, who liked a recent post—that is, they're looking for some type of content. Make sure that the content you create and offer is the content that your users are looking for. Then you can decide how to present the content in a way that will help users reach their goal.

If a wireframe is a skeleton for a user interface, then the content is the internal organs. Just as you might write the HTML for a web page before the CSS, you shouldn't design the frame or structure for your wireframes without knowing what needs to go inside, how important it is, and what purpose it serves.

Separate content from layout

While you don't want to focus on presentation and layout at this point, it isn't too early to start thinking about the information you want to provide and its relative priority in your interface. This is one of the first steps in a process called *content modeling*.

In an article called "How to Use Wireframes for Content Modeling" (https://bkaprt.com/wfe45/02-06) copywriter Derek Gillette wrote:

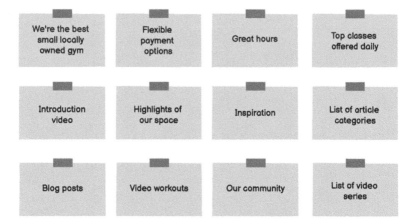

FIG 2.4: These possible features and messages for a gym website can be easily rearranged.

A content model uses blocks (think of these like sticky-notes) to lay out the **must-haves, priorities, and order of the page.** *It will help you to know what needs to be said and in what order, not actual final copy, but the high-level concepts, ideas, and purposes of each section.*

You can do this in a text document or use (real or virtual) sticky notes (**FIG 2.4**). Start by listing all the content that you think should appear on a particular screen.

The next step is to try to arrange the sticky notes in order of importance, from top to bottom (**FIG 2.5**). This will help ensure that your users see the highest priority content first. You'll be surprised by how helpful this can be later, when you're thinking about the exact placement of each element on the screen.

Seeing this list of information in visual blocks helps you imagine how it could flow on a page, and the space it might occupy. Is it too much for one page? If so, "use it to spark a lively internal debate over what HAS to be on the page," Gillette says. Then think about what you might be able to remove or relegate to another page.

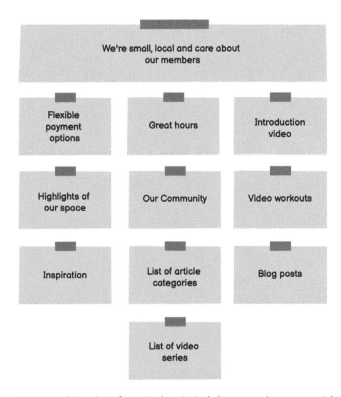

FIG 2.5: Ordering the information by priority helps you see how a user might experience your site.

Feel free to experiment with multiple ideas and send them to stakeholders who you think might have different ideas about what matters most. Better to find out sooner rather than later!

Design from the inside out

We once spoke with a lead developer who was trying to use wireframes to communicate UI designs to other developers on his team. He told us that he had tried wireframing in four separate instances in the past and gave up each time, because his developers misunderstood his designs or focused on the wrong details, like the color of the buttons. But colleagues kept

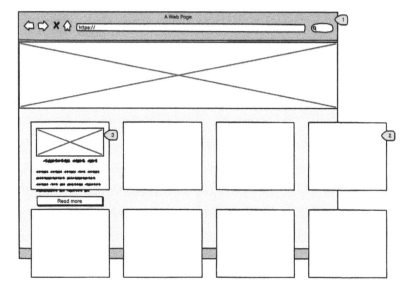

FIG 2.6: Designing outside-in often requires making adjustments later.

encouraging him to create a visual artifact because his text-only specification documents were too long and detailed.

We suggested trying a technique called *inside-out design*. Inside-out design proposes that you start with the lowest-level details first, then gradually expand outward to create parts that make up the whole. Only after all the separate, individual units have been drawn do you draw a box (such as a browser or device window) around the whole thing.

The developer was surprised and confused. He'd been doing the exact opposite—starting with a rectangle of the entire screen first, then adding boxes inside it, then designing inside those boxes—which is very common. Human nature makes us want to put things in boxes—especially when designing *for* boxes, like smartphone and computer screens.

But that approach leaves you focused on layout or implementation before content. Many wireframing tools deliberately leave out precise pixel units or screen dimensions to address this.

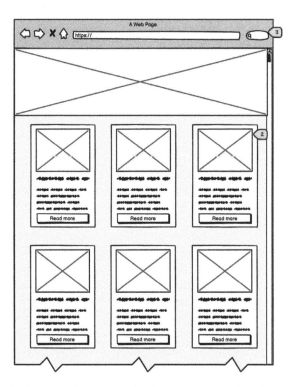

FIG 2.7: Inside-out designing focuses on the smallest unit of content. Once you have that, you can set it to the side for reference while building out the rest of the wireframe.

Let's say you are designing a news site. Traditional outside-in design would wireframe elements in this order: browser window first, then news item containers inside it, then news item details inside those containers (**FIG 2.6**). Your original browser box might not be large enough to fit all the news item containers, which in itself isn't a problem. But the problem is that now you're thinking about the details of the layout, not about the content of the page. It shifts your mindset to closed thinking—getting things to "fit" and look right.

But if you start wireframing the details first, your mindset is different. Inside-out design starts with the smallest unit of content and its container (**FIG 2.7**). Then you can quickly build

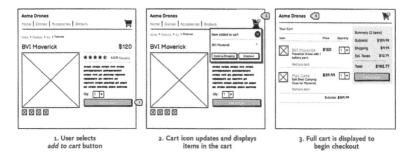

1. User selects *add to cart* **button**

2. Cart icon updates and displays items in the cart

3. Full cart is displayed to begin checkout

FIG 2.8: The checkout experience is critical to the success of an ecommerce site. It's okay to focus on UI details early in one area and hold off on the rest.

the structure around it without fussing over pixel precision. Rather than focusing on box shape and spacing, you're thinking about what goes inside. You ask questions like "How prominent should the image be?" and "Should there be a button or a link to read more?"

If you're designing a content-heavy site or app, you might want to put *only* the content on the screen without any layout elements, so your mind doesn't start trying to fit your content into boxes right away.

Focus on critical interactions

The last technique for building a foundation for your wireframes is to hone in on a cornerstone feature, or step and build around it. Think of a novelist describing a specific character or key event before writing the setup for the novel.

Sometimes getting the experience of a specific interaction *just right* is the best use of your time in the beginning; for example, when your current product has a significant pain point that frustrates your customers or results in high churn.

Digital products created for explicit user tasks or goals—such as placing an order (**FIG 2.8**) or adding a new employee record—often require that critical or time-intensive interactions happen in a specific order. Progression through these steps is an all-or-nothing proposition, resulting in clear success or failure.

Friction at these points in the process can be detrimental to your product's success.

To wireframe these critical interactions first, think about what needs to happen while ignoring how the user got there, and start wireframing from that point in the process. This level of focus is another way of making sure that you prioritize the most important things.

You don't always have to think about the entire flow at the start. By focusing on the screens with key interactions, you can ensure critical steps will get the attention they require as the design progresses.

GENERATING IDEAS

" *Create, then curate.*
Generate tons of ideas. Refine the good ones. Publish only the best ones.
—WRITER DAVID PERELL (https://bkaprt.com/wfe45/02-07)

Once you've laid the foundation with structure and content, it's time to seek success through sheer quantity of ideas, as we've explained previously. At this stage, keep in mind that you aren't designing something that should be considered final in any sense; you're using a design tool to visualize ideas.

It's natural to feel uncomfortable with creating anything rough or imperfect, but that feeling is also completely counter-productive in this phase of design. What's the point of wire-framing an idea that you know is probably *bad*?

For one, you'll learn from it. In *Designing Interfaces*, Jenifer Tidwell wrote, "...in any given project [...] you won't under-stand some design issues until you've designed your way into a dead end." So, your initial idea might be infeasible or just plain wrong, but something worth keeping can—and usually does—emerge from that seed.

All you have to do is stop worrying about having bad ideas! We know this is easier said than done, because so much of our own judgment about what is *good* or *bad* happens sub-consciously. There are a few techniques—using constraints, powering through, and throwing out the rulebook—that we can rely on to encourage creativity and to silence our inner critic. Let's take a closer look at each one.

Use constraints

> *Limitations foster creativity. Tell an artist to paint anything, and he may struggle, but tell him to create something specific, in a set amount of time, for a certain audience, and these constraints might well push him to produce something he might never have come up with on his own.*
> —JOHN C. MCCRAE, WORM (https://bkaprt.com/wfe45/02-08)

A blank canvas comes with infinite possibilities and crushing overwhelm. Introducing constraints can radically alleviate the anxiety of a blank page. Design problems are full of external constraints—the needs of the client, the scope of the project—but self-imposed constraints can make wireframing more creative and productive.

Constraints help you narrow the number of possible design ideas from *everything* to something more manageable. (They also make it easier to ignore how something looks so you can focus instead on how it functions.)

Time constraints

One of the easiest ways to engage your creative mind is to introduce time limits: set a timer, start wireframing, then reset and do it again. And again.

For a single design idea, we recommend that each round should last one to three minutes. The time frame should be short enough for you to feel pressure—forcing you to forgo your more typical thought patterns—yet long enough for you to produce something meaningful or recognizable.

For a single screen or design problem, you will probably start to get diminishing returns at between five and eight iterations. So, restart your timer at least four times before moving on to a different part of the interface or product.

FIG 2.9: An "8-Up" template helps organize rapid idea generation.

We use a simple 8-Up template for this exercise (**FIG 2.9**). Try it out and see if you can come up with eight different ideas in eight minutes!

"What if...?" prompts

Another source of constraints is creative prompts for the design itself. You can create or source a list of prompts in advance using one of many prompt generators online, such as Sharpen's design challenges (https://bkaprt.com/wfe45/02-09). Here are a few of our favorite "What if...?" prompts to get you started:

- What if the product will be used only by people who do not speak the language of the product?
- What if we want our product to be used only by teenagers?
- What if we weren't allowed to use any kind of imagery or visuals?
- What if the product were entirely controlled by voice?
- What if our product had a specific personality (friendly, stoic, quiet, generous, etc.)—what would it look like?

It's okay for the prompts to be impractical, or even silly. The goal isn't to design for that specific scenario but to jolt your brain into a different frame of thinking.

If you want to stay a bit more grounded, focus on all the possible stress cases for your product and optimize for those. A common design mistake is to assume that users are operating in the best-case scenario, which often isn't true. Wireframing for the opposite of ideal can produce thought-provoking choices. In his article, "Design Edge Cases and Where to Find Them," author Tanner Christensen recommends playing with scale as a means of identifying points of stress:

> *When we design, we should consider anything that can be big to be colossal, and anything that can be small as being microscopic. Thinking in such extremes ensures our work will scale, even for situations the team may not be readily accounting for. [...] How do you design for each of these extremes? What happens when the design is carefully crafted for one extreme but not the other end? (https://bkaprt.com/wfe45/02-10)*

"What if...?" prompts that inspire thinking about stress cases might look like this:

- What if a table has ten thousand rows of data?
- What if the internet connection is extremely slow or unreliable?
- What if users are on the smallest device out there?
- What if all the content is translated into German (or a similarly long-worded language)?
- What if the user has all of their font sizes doubled?

"What if...?" scenarios have the dual benefit of giving your creativity a jolt and prompting you to consider real situations in which your users might use your product. They can help catch design or technical problems before any code has been written.

"How might we...?" questions

Another way of introducing constraints is to reframe your understanding of the problem. Asking and answering "How might we...?" questions can elicit new ideas that wouldn't be otherwise obvious.

Let's say an organization is struggling to increase subscriber numbers. It would be perfectly logical to begin your wireframe session by framing the problem as, "Get more people to click the Signup button on the website," and then try to improve the website from there. But problem statements are narrow by necessity and may yield only a few narrow solutions to a broader problem.

Instead, asking *"How might we* increase the number of subscribers?" can prompt different solutions that go beyond the Signup button on the website. You might start to think about designing landing pages for new audiences that you are trying to attract, improving the experience of the signup flow, or adding a feature to allow existing customers to refer new customers within the product.

The phrase "How might we...?" frees you up to entertain so many more possibilities, which is the ideal state of mind during this phase of the design process.

Power through

Using constraints helps you trick yourself into being creative, which is a great way to start. But, like most worthwhile efforts, sometimes you just have to face the challenge head-on.

Research actually backs this up. In her book, *Continuous Discovery Habits*, author Teresa Torres summarized several key findings on creativity, stating (https://bkaprt.com/wfe45/02-11):

> [T]he more original ideas tend to be generated toward the end of the ideation session. [...] [W]e want to learn to keep the loop open longer. We want to learn to push beyond our first mediocre and obvious ideas, and delve into the realm of more diverse, original ideas.

Powering through—pushing beyond your first few ideas—is a simple technique, but it's not easy. When you've sketched out your initial ideas and feel like you want to move on, push yourself to create *just one more*. And really go for it—make one last sketch that's more novel or "out there" than the others so far.

It's a bit like athletic training. The biggest gains come from what's left after you think you've given all you can.

In addition to coming up with more novel ideas, pushing past the obvious gives you more ideas to build from. The broader your range of ideas, the more possibilities emerge. Adding just one more idea early on might spawn five or more ideas later, as ideas have a way of propagating and branching out from one another. Don't stop once you've found one or even a few good solutions; exploring a bit further might land you a maximally better one.

Throw away the rulebook

Essential to most design methodologies, is, well, method. Or, at least some kind of procedure or framework to follow as you develop the design. And sure, we've spent a lot of time talking about problem statements, techniques, flows, and constraints. But this chapter is also about getting started. Being fruitful. Relishing possibility!

In these early design phases, you're just trying to get the ideas out of your head and onto the screen as fast as possible. Do whatever helps you do that, regardless of what it looks like or whether it has a proven set of rules.

Don't limit yourself to boxes, lines, and premade UI components. Branch out into text, sticky notes, screenshots, and heck, even inspirational images. Nothing you include is wrong; it's okay for your ideas to look more like a collage than a product at this point (**FIG 2.10**).

Collecting elements for your collage might also inspire you to borrow from others (though we don't *actually* recommend stealing from or copying others' work). But you can certainly draw on the experience of other practitioners' solutions for solving a similar problem to yours (a.k.a., don't reinvent the wheel) (**FIG 2.11**).

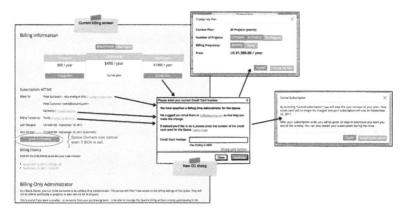

FIG 2.10: Combining screenshots and wireframes is one of the fastest ways to sketch out new functionality while providing context within an existing product.

And don't forget to also look outside your specialty, or your industry entirely. You'll be surprised by how successfully ideas can be applied across wildly different fields (**FIG 2.12**).

Remember, early wireframes are just for you, and maybe a few people on your team. Approach this stage with a flexible and fluid mindset; what makes them "good" right now is how well they facilitate productive conversations.

TAKE STOCK

As you explore early ideas, it's very likely that you'll get stuck somewhere, or you'll mentally flag a few ideas to come back to later. That's okay. Once you exhaust your creativity, you can take some time to go back and review.

If you get stuck along the way, it probably means there are unanswered questions. Use this stopping point to gather answers to those questions, either from existing research you've done or by asking a subject matter expert or stakeholder. If you want to revisit your flagged ideas, spend a bit of time noting details or next steps you might need to take to develop them further.

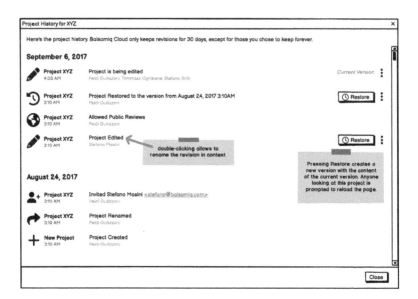

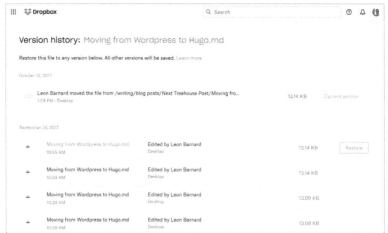

FIG 2.11: Restoring files isn't a new problem, so when Balsamiq wanted to add a feature to support version control, we looked to Dropbox because they'd already designed a great solution.

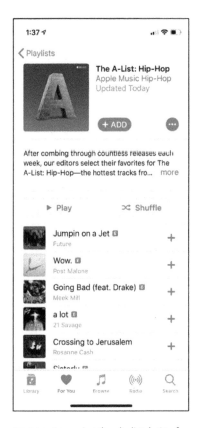
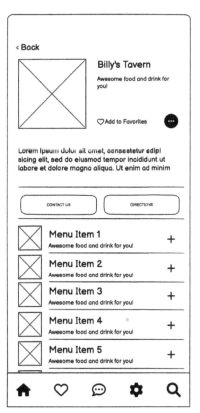

FIG 2.12: Borrowing the playlist design from a music app serves as inspiration for a food ordering app.

You'll know you're on the right track if you have a lot of great ideas and a few terrible ones. It's still too early to pick a single design and start building, but you can narrow it down to some of your most promising ideas and discard the weaker ones. Just make sure you're left with several different wireframes worth developing further—because that's what comes next.

3 FROM IDEAS TO INTERFACES

BY NOW YOU'VE GOT SEVERAL rough wireframe ideas that you're eager to develop further. The next step is to start constructing user interfaces—screens, pages, or displays—for your product, using—you guessed it—wireframes! In this chapter, we're going to explore the elements used to assemble an interface and how to communicate them through wireframes.

The first thing to understand when learning interface design is that your users encounter dozens of other user interfaces daily, which become a reference for any new product they encounter. For better or worse, users want new products to behave according to their expectations, based on how other products work—a concept known as *Jakob's Law of Internet User Experience* (https://bkaprt.com/wfe45/03-01).

You can make a product more effective by following conventions and best practices. Even if you're creating a totally new type of product, you can still use established interface patterns and behaviors, taking advantage of Jakob's Law to help your new idea feel familiar. This will allow users to focus on their goals without having to learn a new set of rules.

FIG 3.1: Shopping website interfaces are made up of many different design elements (highlighted in blue), from menu bars to icons to thumbnail images.

ANATOMY OF A USER INTERFACE

Let's start our understanding of user interfaces by looking at how they're built. You've likely visited hundreds of shopping websites in your life (**FIG 3.1**), but have you ever thought about why they were designed that way (aside from making that "add to cart" button big and bold, of course)?

It's fascinating to think that UI designers deliberately chose each element on the page—to make up the collection of UI building blocks—including their size and placement. Every menu, button, link, and image has a specific purpose, and good UI designers choose these elements carefully, in the same way a poet might choose among similar words, each with a slightly different connotation or tone.

If you've followed our guidance in the previous chapter on using wireframes to generate rough ideas, then you may have a lot of concepts that don't really look like a product

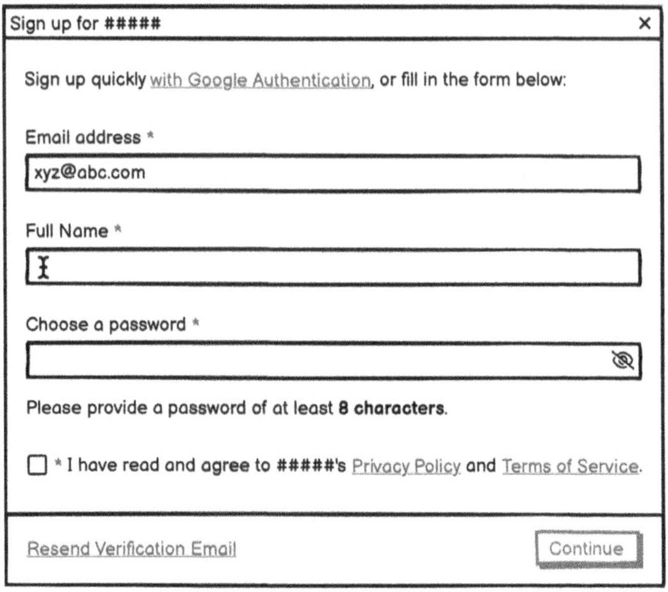

| Sign up for ##### | ✕ |

Sign up quickly with Google Authentication, or fill in the form below:

Email address *

xyz@abc.com

Full Name *

Choose a password *

👁̸

Please provide a password of at least **8 characters**.

☐ * I have read and agree to #####'s Privacy Policy and Terms of Service.

Resend Verification Email   Continue

FIG. 3.2: Forms are one of the most common patterns in UI design.

yet—that's good! Wireframe sketches should consist of a lot of shapes (boxes, arrows, simple icons) and maybe some words to describe them. What we want to do now is turn those shapes into interface "objects" (we'll get into specific terminology soon) based on their function or purpose.

The shapes in your wireframe all represent *components* in your user interface, which become *patterns* when combined, which further combine into *page templates*. For example, a signup form combines components like text, input fields, and buttons to create a reusable pattern (**FIG 3.2**). Let's look at how to identify and choose the right interface elements for your wireframes.

COMPONENTS

Components (or *controls*) are the basic building blocks of all user interfaces. They vary in user-facing appearance and behavior, but we define them as the lowest-level elements or objects in code. Most interfaces use dozens of components, but we'll focus on the most common components for now—text, buttons and links, and selection components. Once you understand and use these, you'll be able to adopt others without much trouble.

Text

From headlines to input field labels, text is the most important component because it says everything (literally). Your customer won't know what to do if you design a button with no text—and they certainly won't *click or tap it*. The only thing an unlabeled input field will prompt is frustration.

It's important to understand what kinds of text elements you need, and where they'll be most effective, to ensure a product's usability. Here are the most important types of interface text:

- **Page titles or headings.** These help users identify where they are in the experience and provide a quick way to reach the main sections of a website. Always place the title or heading at the top of the page, and include only one main heading per page (**FIG 3.3**).
- **Body or main text.** This refers to longer portions of text that are used for explanations or narratives. Split up body text with paragraph breaks and headings, to avoid a "wall of text" that can be hard to scan.
- **Labels.** Short pieces of text placed above an input component communicate what information is being requested. Your label can echo the component name, which is common.
- **Helper text.** This is text within an input field used to suggest acceptable or suitable terms for the particular input. Show an example of an expected search term to give the user a starting point.
- **Tool tips.** Tool-tip text is brief, triggered by a user interaction such as hovering over a Help icon (**FIG 3.4**). Use tool

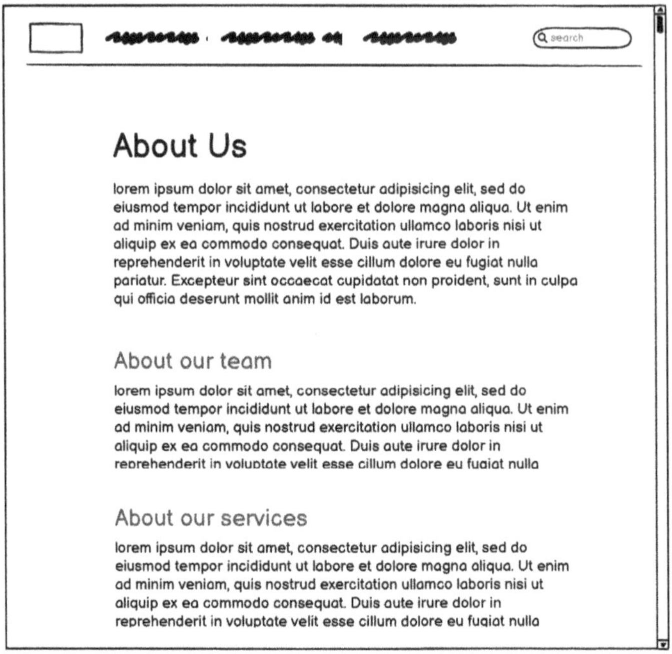

About Us

lorem ipsum dolor sit amet, consectetur adipisicing elit, sed do eiusmod tempor incididunt ut labore et dolore magna aliqua. Ut enim ad minim veniam, quis nostrud exercitation ullamco laboris nisi ut aliquip ex ea commodo consequat. Duis aute irure dolor in reprehenderit in voluptate velit esse cillum dolore eu fugiat nulla pariatur. Excepteur sint occaecat cupidatat non proident, sunt in culpa qui officia deserunt mollit anim id est laborum.

About our team

lorem ipsum dolor sit amet, consectetur adipisicing elit, sed do eiusmod tempor incididunt ut labore et dolore magna aliqua. Ut enim ad minim veniam, quis nostrud exercitation ullamco laboris nisi ut aliquip ex ea commodo consequat. Duis aute irure dolor in reprehenderit in voluptate velit esse cillum dolore eu fugiat nulla

About our services

lorem ipsum dolor sit amet, consectetur adipisicing elit, sed do eiusmod tempor incididunt ut labore et dolore magna aliqua. Ut enim ad minim veniam, quis nostrud exercitation ullamco laboris nisi ut aliquip ex ea commodo consequat. Duis aute irure dolor in reprehenderit in voluptate velit esse cillum dolore eu fugiat nulla

FIG 3.3: If you want users to read what's on your page, use headings of different sizes to convey the outline of the document and adequate spacing between them.

tips to provide even further context for the meaning of an input component.

Text makes up the majority of most interfaces and can make or break their usability. You don't need final copy in the early designs, but getting a strong grasp of the role and type of text in the interface is valuable at any phase.

Buttons and links

Buttons and links allow users to take action or navigate within, or away from, your application. Since they have the power to prompt actions that can take the user away from where they

FIG 3.4: This example of a tool tip helps users by answering the most common support questions.

are, make your buttons and links clear and prominent. Only use them to provide realistic options to users.

There are three types of buttons you can incorporate into your wireframe:

- A *primary button* (sometimes referred to as a *call to action*) is styled prominently to indicate the desired action. Present only one primary button at a time on screen to avoid confusing or distracting your user.
- You may need to provide users with additional actions they can take. If so, style *secondary buttons* differently than primary buttons to make them appear lower in the visual hierarchy (**FIG 3.5**).

Reply to Comment

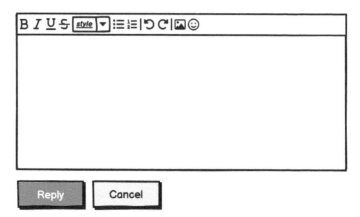

- Text that behaves as a button is considered a *text button*. Use text buttons for less prominent actions or elements on the page (**FIG 3.6**), or when multiple actions have similar levels of importance.

While buttons sometimes link to other sections or sites, it's uncommon for links to function as buttons. *Links* are represented by simple text, styled to indicate interactivity (**FIG 3.7**). Links use different colored text and underlining to provide visual clues that they're clickable or tappable.

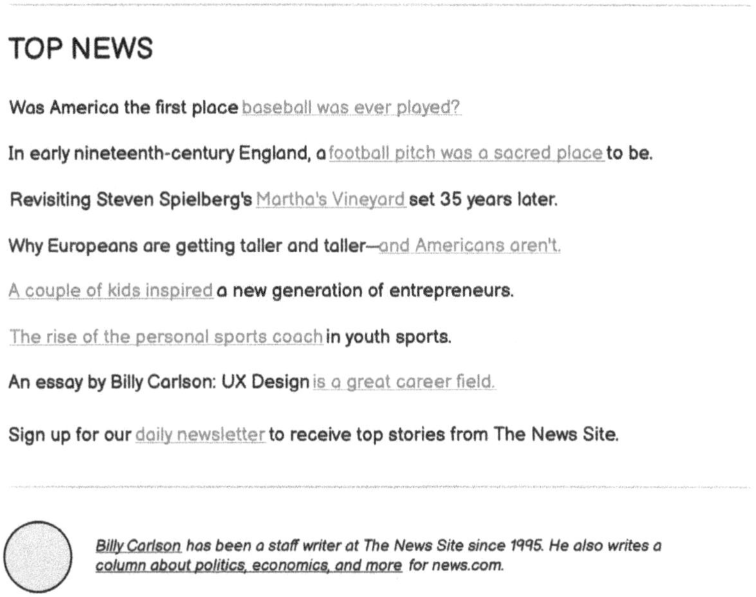

TOP NEWS

Was America the first place baseball was ever played?

In early nineteenth-century England, a football pitch was a sacred place to be.

Revisiting Steven Spielberg's Martha's Vineyard set 35 years later.

Why Europeans are getting taller and taller—and Americans aren't.

A couple of kids inspired a new generation of entrepreneurs.

The rise of the personal sports coach in youth sports.

An essay by Billy Carlson: UX Design is a great career field.

Sign up for our daily newsletter to receive top stories from The News Site.

Billy Carlson has been a staff writer at The News Site since 1995. He also writes a column about politics, economics, and more for news.com.

FIG 3.7: News websites use links to highlight related content throughout and at the end of each article. Using a link for only the most important part of the text is more effective than linking an entire sentence.

In practice, the line between buttons and links has blurred as web and desktop patterns have converged. Rather than try to determine and follow the industry standard, use them consistently within your product. If you're unsure whether to use buttons, links, or both, there are several factors to consider (**FIG 3.8**):

Selection components

Selection components (or simply, *selectors*) help users execute more complex interactions. For example, buying a movie ticket requires searching and filtering lists of movies, choosing the number of tickets, selecting seats, and going through a purchase flow. Each step needs different interactive elements for a smooth experience.

	BUTTONS	LINKS
Use case	Actions like submitting a form, saving progress, and activating modals	Navigating around websites and apps and going to other pages
Placement	Must appear as a design element separate from the main text	Can appear anywhere, including in line with the main text
Text	Clear, brief text	Longer, more descriptive text

FIG 3.8: Buttons and links each have unique considerations when it comes to use case, placement, and text type.

Here are the most common types of selectors:

- **Radio buttons.** These are for when users can only choose one option at a time. Think of their function like picking a radio station to listen to (FIG 3.9).
- **Checkboxes.** This type of component allows users to select multiple options at once. (FIG 3.10).
- **Dropdowns.** A dropdown menu lets users select an item from a predefined list. Dropdowns save space by hiding all options until opened (FIG 3.11).
- **Tags.** This option helps users find content by topic, type, or category through keywords. Tags are especially effective for finding new or related content among a voluminous (or indeterminate) set of options (FIG 3.12).

For all types of selection components, provide a default choice, when possible, to save users time and thought. In some cases, you can predict the most common selection, or what choice(s) a user will make. When you can't, choose a default based on selections made most often or recently (FIG 3.13). However, always base your default choices on the user's desires, not yours (defaulting to the most expensive shipping option, for example, might be your marketing team's preference, but it's inconsiderate and manipulative for customers).

Shipping Address 12 Waldo Point Road, Mishauken, NY 11200   <u>Edit</u>

Shipping Method

⦿ UPS Ground	$2.20
○ UPS 3 Day Select	$5.50
○ UPS 2nd Day Air	$9.50
○ UPS Next Day Air	$12.50

< Return to Customer Information   Continue to Payment Method

FIG 3.9: Radio buttons help users select only one among several available options.

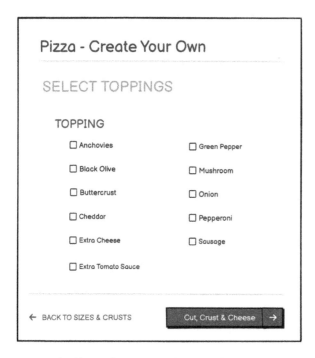

FIG 3.10: Checkboxes allow users to select several options at once, for instance when ordering, because sometimes they want many or all options, or even none.

FIG 3.11: Dropdowns are used in forms when space is at a premium and the number of choices is more than three.

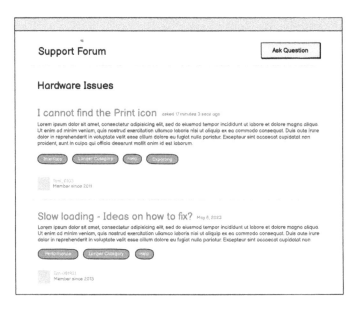

FIG 3.12: Forum websites use tags on each post to help users find or discover topic categories when searching for an answer to a question.

FIG 3.13: An example of making a default selection based on the last-used viewer.

The best way to learn how to use UI components is to observe them in your day-to-day interactions with them. Pay attention to how other sites and products implement them, and reflect on what works well and what doesn't. You'll soon develop opinions that you can put into practice in your wireframes.

PATTERNS

A user interface pattern is a reusable group of UI components (buttons, labels, checkboxes, links, etc.) that solve a specific problem. What distinguishes patterns from components is that components usually don't do anything by themselves. You may write a message in a text box, but the desired action results from combining the contents of that text box with the Send button to deliver it.

Patterns can consist of as few as two components, or up to a dozen or more. They are distinguished by their focus on

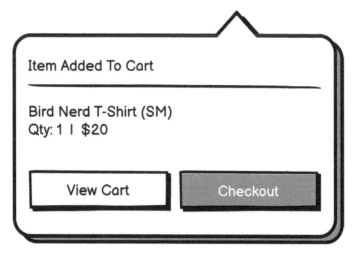

FIG 3.14: Even a small ecommerce shopping cart overlay is a pattern, because it's repeated across the site.

fulfilling one primary function, such as navigating the main categories on a site, filtering search results, selecting a size option, or entering credit card information. They rarely occupy an entire screen, which is typically made of up of multiple patterns.

You might even have a design pattern library to refer to (this could be in your design system, UI framework, or stylesheet), in which case your job in this phase is to identify the best patterns to use and indicate them in your wireframes.

A pattern that you might see on a shopping site is a *cart preview overlay* (**FIG 3.14**), consisting of text and buttons. While the content varies, depending on what's in the user's cart, the overall pattern is reused throughout the site.

There are many patterns in the world of user interface design—the website, UI Patterns (https://bkaprt.com/wfe45/03-02), lists well over 100—so we can't cover them all here. But they generally fall into three categories: *navigation*, *content*, and *input*. Knowing how to pick and use the most common patterns in these categories will help you take your wireframes from an exercise in problem-solving to a blueprint for implementation.

Navigation patterns

Navigation patterns exist to help users move around your site or application. *Primary navigation* (sometimes called *global navigation* or *main menu*) is the central method for navigating a site or app. It serves as a wayfinding anchor point and is persistent throughout the experience. For any reasonably complex application or site, you'll probably also need *secondary navigation*, which allows for navigation within a top-level category, as well as navigation elements like *breadcrumbs* and *footers*.

The breadth and depth of the sitemap—the relationships between pages or screens—should determine the type of navigation pattern to use. Don't choose a navigation pattern until you have at least a general idea of the breadth and depth of your entire product.

Fortunately, the rules are straightforward from there:

- Use vertical (i.e., narrow) navigation if your navigation structure is broad (i.e., there are many, or potentially many, items to choose from).
- Use horizontal (i.e., wide) navigation if your navigation is limited to a handful (precise, we know!) of items.

We see examples of this in applications and products we use every day, such as the horizontal file menu and vertical folder structure used by desktop operating systems for decades (**FIG 3.15**).

In her course "How to Design Navigation for Large and Small Screens" (https://bkaprt.com/wfe45/03-03), designer Donna Spencer explains the most common horizontal and vertical navigation patterns and provides great wireframe examples to learn from, which we'll use in this section.

Horizonal navigation

The first and most common horizontal navigation pattern is an inline list (or *bar*) of menu items, which can be styled as basic shapes, tabs, or text links (**FIG 3.16**). Separate items sufficiently so that users can easily click on their desired target. Make active

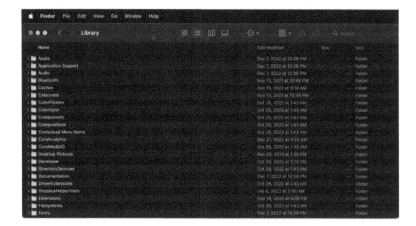

FIG 3.15: The macOS Finder application shows menu actions across the top of the screen and folder navigation items vertically down the screen. It wouldn't work the other way around.

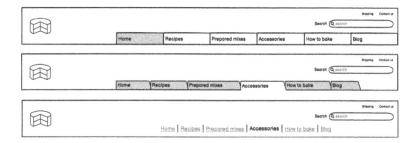

FIG 3.16: A flat (single-level) menu bar, shown in multiple variations.

or selected items clear. For products with a flat navigation structure, this may be the only navigation you need.

Menu bars also work for mobile devices or websites, with a few differences; namely, they can reside at the top or bottom of the screen. They also can't fit as many items across the screen (ideally four or fewer, to allow for easy targeting). It's acceptable, but not preferable, to use horizontal scrolling or a "more" menu to show the items that don't fit in the default viewport (**FIG 3.17**).

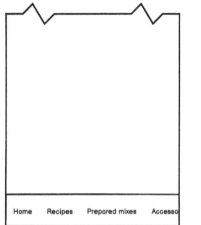 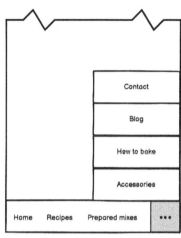

FIG 3.17: Two options for showing additional menu items on a mobile screen: horizontal scrolling (left) or nesting them in an additional menu (right).

Since horizontal navigation is used pretty much everywhere in web and desktop applications, it's easy to find examples and inspiration for the problem you're trying to solve. But keep in mind that horizontal navigation is both prominently located and persists across screens. The more space and weight it carries, the more attention it takes away from the rest of the screen, which is the part that really matters to your user.

The goal of horizontal navigation isn't to provide a way for your users to get *everywhere* from *anywhere* in a single click, it's to help direct them to get where they want to go by providing signposts and directions, the same way highway signs list only the main destinations rather than every exit along the way. (For more about how to choose menu depth and breadth, Lisa Maria Marquis has an entire chapter dedicated to site structure in her book, *Everyday Information Architecture*.)

Vertical navigation

Now, on to vertical navigation. Most vertical navigation is a flat or nested list of items in a sidebar, placed on either the left or

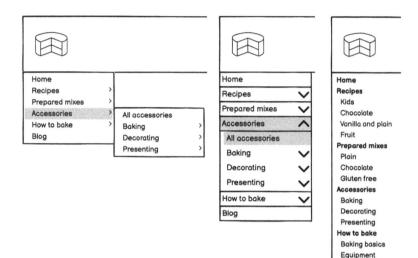

FIG 3.18: Nested levels can expand out to the side as an overlay (left), expand within the side navigation panel (center), or show the entire hierarchy if it's not too long (right).

the right of the screen (usually the left, in cultures that read left to right, although it's more flexible when it comes to mobile navigation).

Vertical navigation works well when you have a large or indeterminate number of items in your navigation structure. Its placement and orientation offer space for many more items than a menu bar and support hierarchical navigation well.

Vertical navigation can show multilevel navigation structures (primary and secondary together) in more ways than horizontal navigation can. Because its scrolling is more common and intuitive, you can put more items in a vertical structure. For example, there are at least three ways to show a hierarchical menu using vertical navigation: overlays, collapsible groups (also called accordions), or fully expanded lists (**FIG 3.18**).

Mobile choices are similar, except they're typically hidden by default. You're probably familiar with the ubiquitous "hamburger" menu pattern that reveals vertical navigation, either by

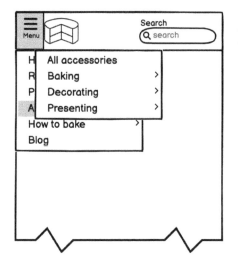

FIG 3.19: Make sure that your mobile overlay menus are well organized. Otherwise, they can be hard to use.

sliding the content to the right or via an overlay with overlapping subnavigation (**FIG 3.19**).

When creating your vertical menus, don't take advantage of this flexibility to include everything without thinking it through. And keep in mind that side navigation and the content next to it will always compete for attention.

Secondary navigation

If your menu items have nested items, you have a few options. If you only have two levels of navigation hierarchy *and* the second levels don't have many items, then you can add a second level of horizontal navigation to your menu bar (**FIG 3.20**). Make sure to keep the top-level category shown as highlighted or selected as well as the second-level menu item.

If you have two or more levels of navigation hierarchy and any of the subsequent levels have more than a handful of items, then you can add a dropdown (a.k.a., "hover" or "flyout") menu to your menu bar, combining horizontal navigation with vertical, which is frequently used for secondary navigation (**FIG 3.21**).

FIG 3.20: A two-level menu bar.

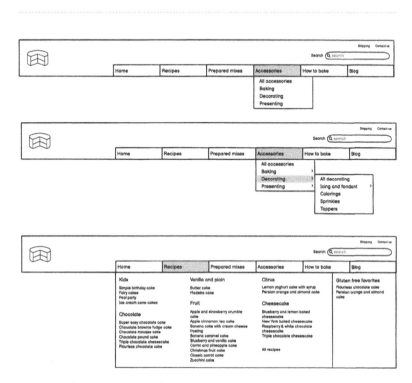

FIG 3.21: Multilevel menu bars with two and more levels of hierarchy, plus a "mega menu" that is even more flexible.

To understand the difference between secondary and primary vertical navigation, remember that primary navigation allows you to go to all the main categories of the site and stays the same across all pages of the site. Secondary vertical navigation is *local* (showing only the items within the selected primary menu) and *contextual* (its contents change based on which top-level category you are in).

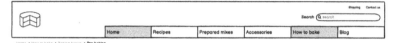

Pre baking

FIG 3.22: Breadcrumbs used to show navigation back to the root of the hierarchy.

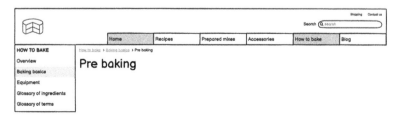

FIG 3.23: Breadcrumbs used to show navigation back to the top-level navigation category only.

The advantage of using vertical navigation as supporting navigation is that it's familiar and flexible. It's also compact and can remain visible, unlike a hover menu, so that users can easily see where they are at a glance.

When using secondary vertical navigation, make sure that it appears below the primary horizontal navigation. Otherwise, users could mistake it for primary navigation.

Breadcrumbs

Another popular type of supporting navigation is *breadcrumbs*, which show users what section and what, if any, subsections of the site or product they're in. They are usually styled simply, such as text links with an arrow between them.

You can use breadcrumbs as secondary navigation by showing the global hierarchy (**FIG 3.22**), or as tertiary navigation by showing only the local hierarchy (**FIG 3.23**) when combined with secondary vertical navigation.

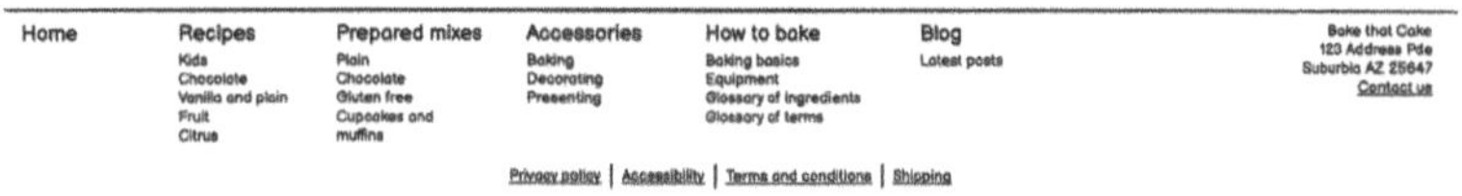

Home	Recipes	Prepared mixes	Accessories	How to bake	Blog		Bake that Cake
	Kids	Plain	Baking	Baking basics	Latest posts		123 Address Pde
	Chocolate	Chocolate	Decorating	Equipment			Suburbia AZ 25647
	Vanilla and plain	Gluten free	Presenting	Glossary of ingredients			Contact us
	Fruit	Cupcakes and		Glossary of terms			
	Citrus	muffins					

Privacy policy | Accessibility | Terms and conditions | Shipping

FIG 3.24: You can put navigation, plus necessary supplemental information, inside a website footer.

Breadcrumbs should always show the name of the currently selected page as the final item in the breadcrumb list, but only as text, not as a linked item. Always repeat the name of the page below the breadcrumbs; breadcrumb text is often small, so don't rely on it to tell users where they are.

Footer navigation

Another form of supporting navigation is with *footer navigation*. A footer is a delineated area of a site that sits at the bottom of every page. Its advantages are that it consumes the full width of the page and, because it doesn't obscure any content below it, footer navigation doesn't need to be as compact as primary horizontal navigation.

Footer navigation is often shown in the same way that a horizontal "mega menu" might appear, with the addition of supplemental information about the site or company, such as legal or contact information (FIG 3.24).

Treat footer navigation as the navigation of last resort. Users will often look in the footer when they can't find what they are looking for anywhere else. So, if you want your users to find something specific, make sure it's also easy to find near the top of the page.

While you don't need to address navigation patterns in your wireframes first, it can be a useful way to set the foundation for content patterns and plan out the space you'll have available for them. Let's dig into those now.

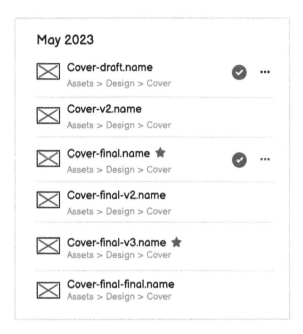

FIG 3.25: A file storage app may contain a list of file names along with multiple status indicators.

Content patterns

Content patterns hold multiples pieces of information, or information that is presented in multiple formats (text, icons, images, etc.). There are many, but you can get a lot of mileage out of just a few common ones—lists, tables, and tiles and cards.

Lists

Lists are best for showing content that needs to be, well, listed. They allow users to easily scan a collection of similar items and select an individual item to explore further if needed. Lists are good for large or unknown quantities of brief information, such as file names or email subjects. They are versatile and sometimes contain more than just text, such as icons for additional actions (**FIG 3.25**).

| Auth type: | Any ▾ | | | Export 🖶 |

☐	API ▲	Description	Auth	HTTPS	Link
☐	Charity Search	Nonprofit charity data	apiKey	No	visit
☐	Clearbit Logo API	Search for company logos and embed them in your projects	No	Yes	visit
☐	Domainsdb.info	Registered domain names search	No	Yes	visit
☐	Gmail	Flexible, RESTful access to the user's inbox	OAuth	Yes	visit
☐	Google Analytics	Collect, configure, and analyze your data to reach the right audi	OAuth	Yes	visit
☐	markerapi	Trademark Search	No	No	visit
☐	Trello	Boards, lists, and cards to help you organize and prioritize your	OAuth	Yes	visit

« ‹ 1 of 3 › »

FIG 3.26: Tables are for data, but you can also use them to present other complex information in an organized way.

Tables

Tables are used for data sets that have multiple dimensions (**FIG 3.26**). In addition to showing multiple pieces of information for each item, they can also have actions associated with one or more rows of information (such as edit, delete, or export).

When you present information in a table, first consider what information is most important and what can possibly be left out or relegated to a child page. Next, you can highlight key values or critical thresholds with bold and/or colored text. Last, rather than thinking about what information you can or want to present, ask yourself what the user wants to do with it and optimize around that.

Tiles and cards

Tiles are rows and/or columns of images that allow viewers to quickly browse lists of primarily visual content (**FIG 3.27**). Use them when the imagery or other visual elements alone convey enough information to describe and distinguish each item. Tiles often scroll within a row or column, or have a fixed number of items in one dimension which wraps along the other dimension.

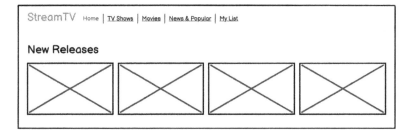

FIG 3.27: Streaming video services often use tiles to facilitate the browsing experience.

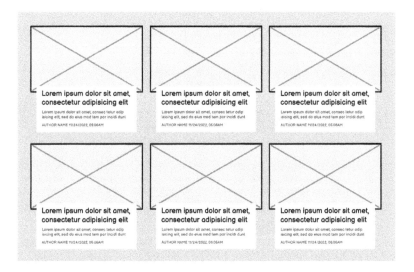

FIG 3.28: A news website might use cards to allow users to easily scan their articles.

Cards present both visual and textual information in a relatively compact format, and scale well as a grid on a variety of screen sizes, although unlike tiles, they typically don't scroll horizontally. Cards feature a prominent image like tiles, but also include various text elements such as a title, subtitle, description, and other components such as links and buttons (**FIG 3.28**). This makes them a bit more versatile than tiles, but also more complex.

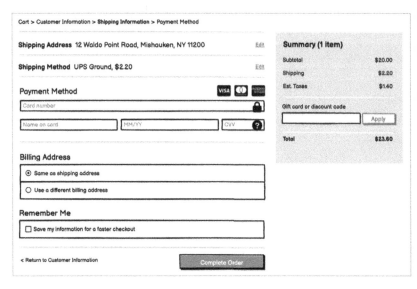

FIG 3.29: Forms typically combine all the components we described earlier—text, buttons (and sometimes links), and selection controls—into one powerful pattern.

Lists, tiles, and cards work best when each piece of information is the same or similar in size or length. Their similarity makes them easy to scan and parse, so you should be familiar with the expected content before wireframing.

Let the content dictate the type of pattern to use. For example, forcing long text blocks into a list or card will make it difficult to read. Similarly, if you plan to overlay text on top of images, use sufficient contrast to make it readable.

Input patterns

Use input patterns when you're asking the user to provide information or make a decision. They may contain some content and even some navigation, but their primary purpose is to collect user input in order to decide what to do or show next. Common input patterns include forms, modals and prompts, and search bars and filters.

Forms

We all use forms on a regular basis: to purchase things through checkout flows (**FIG 3.29**), to provide information when opening an account or updating a profile, and to transmit secure financial data. And they all seem to ask for too much information and never seem to work the same way. Remember that pain when planning your forms!

In most cases, you'll know when you need a form. The tricky part is knowing what and where to put the various components. When designing forms:

- **Only ask for information you absolutely need.** The more information a person must fill out, the less likely they will be to fill it out completely or correctly. When creating a signup form, you shouldn't need to ask for a person's full name, address, or phone number, for example. If you need that information for personalization, you can ask for it after they have signed up, such as on a Profile or Account screen.
- **If you need to gather a lot of information from a user, break up the form into logical steps.** You see this often when checking out from an online retailer: first you fill out your personal information. Next, you tell them where and how you want to ship the product. And finally, you fill out payment information to complete the purchase. You'll often do these tasks on separate pages or separate accordions.
- **Use adequate spacing to improve readability.** A good guideline for new or non-designers is to double the amount of whitespace you think you need everywhere on the page. This is especially applicable to forms, which are often densely packed. Users usually don't mind scrolling through lengthy information if it's presented and designed well.
- **One column is better than two.** Again, it may seem like a waste of space to not spread form fields across two columns when you have room, but human eyes are used to scanning horizontally before moving downward, so disrupting that process can be disorienting and confusing.

- **Use label placement intentionally.** Putting labels above form fields is often the easiest for users to follow the flow of information. But for longer forms, placing the labels to the left of the fields (in left-to-right written languages) can save space without resulting in too much added complexity. Don't place labels inside form fields, because they can disappear when the user starts typing. Make labels visible to users at all times.

It's hard to get forms right, so don't spend too much time trying to make them perfect in this phase. You'll have time to ask for help later.

Modals and prompts

Modal windows (or *modals*) are often used to promote content or prompt users with questions. You may be familiar with modals by their other name, *popups*, as they interrupt the main experience by obscuring and temporarily disabling the content behind them. Modals facilitate tasks that a user might need to take before moving on to a new or subsequent part of the experience.

A modal may also be referred to as a *prompt* (**FIG 3.30**) when its purpose to is ask the user a question, either to get more information or to notify the user of a change to the system before continuing.

Here are a few tips for designing modals and prompts:

- **Use plain language.** Avoid using jargon to explain why you're interrupting the user or why you're asking them a question. Be brief and straightforward.
- **Follow conventions for button placement and layout.** The user should know exactly how to take action. When in doubt, assign the default button to the *least destructive* action. When faced with a choice about deleting all of their data, for example, you don't want your users to make a big decision thoughtlessly.

FIG 3.30: An example prompt to alert the user that they are about to take an irreversible action.

FIG 3.31: Make search fields obvious through icons and text inside or next to them.

Users can get annoyed with modals and prompts. They're distracting and break the user's attention, so use them only when necessary.

Search bars and filters

Search bars are simple input fields that reveal a powerful tool. Effective search allows users to get where they need to go. If your product has search functionality, it should be omnipresent. Place it prominently at the top of the site.

Don't overthink or get too playful with the design of your search field. Its behavior and purpose should be clear. People will look for an outlined input field paired with the word *search* and possibly a magnifying glass icon (**FIG 3.31**).

You can also include helper text within the search field to give the user suggestions about what is searchable. Adding predictive text like Google does, or autocomplete, can help users refine their query to get the best results (**FIG 3.32**). These little

FIG 3.32: Google uses predictive text to suggest searchable options to the user as they type.

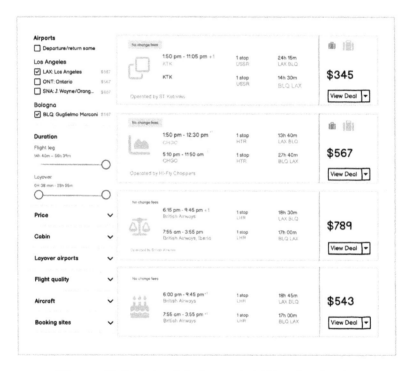

FIG 3.33: Filters are effective for travel sites because the initial number of results can be very high. Some sites will collapse less frequently used options, using an accordion component, to prevent cognitive overload.

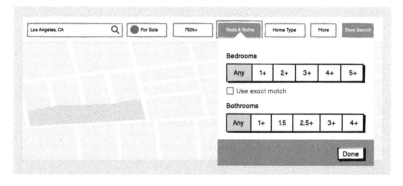

FIG 3.34: Real estate filtering options take into account that, when looking for a home, most people are primarily interested in location, price, and size.

assists can go a long way in making your product feel intuitive and trustworthy.

Filters are another powerful tool to help users find the content they want. They use selection components to sort through the results of a search, or to browse within a category, by narrowing parameters (**FIG 3.33**).

Search and filters work in tandem to give users the ability to wade through large amounts of data or content through a variety of UI components (**FIG 3.34**). When determining the placement of your search and filter patterns, follow similar rules to navigation patterns. If you have a limited number of filters, you can place them horizontally across the top of the page so that they remain prominent and easy to access. When there are many filtering options (think Amazon, eBay, or any large online shopping website), placing the search and filter functionality vertically on the side is more practical (**FIG 3.35**).

When designing filters:

- **Group filtering options by type**, e.g., Price, Brand, Rating. This allows the user to easily scan what is filterable.
- **Display which filters have been applied, and which haven't.** Users should know at a glance whether they're seeing all items or only a subset.

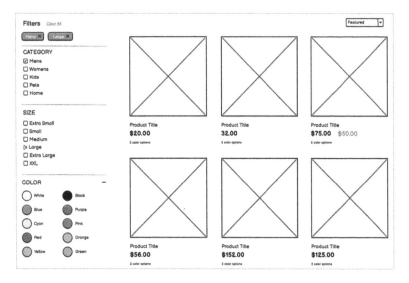

FIG 3.35: In ecommerce sites, filters are often positioned on one side of the screen, next to product previews.

FIG 3.36: Whether you're choosing a new album to listen to in the Music app (left) or a new podcast to listen to in the Podcast app (right), you can recognize the design template Apple uses in its applications.

- **Provide the ability to quickly clear all applied filters**. This allows users to quickly reset or start over.

Filters are both powerful and common. But they can also get complex very quickly, so look for standard practices elsewhere before starting from scratch.

Creating and reusing patterns is one of the most effective ways to provide a good experience for your users—especially repeat users who gain familiarity with them—and to save time and effort for developers, who can use the same tested code snippets across the product.

PAGE TEMPLATES

Once you've wireframed some pages with groups of components and patterns that you like, you can start thinking about page templates. *Page templates* (or, simply *templates*) are collections of patterns that represent types of pages or screens in an app or product, such as a homepage, category pages, or product detail pages.

You can even use templates across applications. Launch an app that comes preinstalled with macOS and you may see repeated templates and patterns (**FIG 3.36**). This makes it easier to learn and use a new app in the same product suite or family.

Templates are meant to be repeatable across many pages, so that even websites consisting of hundreds or thousands of pages typically use fewer than ten templates. This helps designers avoid having to create and manage hundreds of possible layouts, and a template's familiarity helps users understand your product more efficiently.

Consider your favorite blog. The homepage might use a unique template to highlight popular content and entice new visitors to spend time reading. It also might contain a category page template listing all the posts, likely filterable by date or category type. The site might reuse the category page template for a search results page or advertiser's section. Every blog post probably uses the same blog post template. Even though the

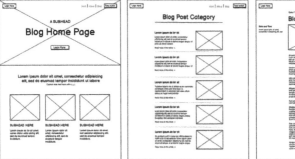

FIG 3.37: Sample templates for a blog site's homepage (left), category page (middle), and post page (right).

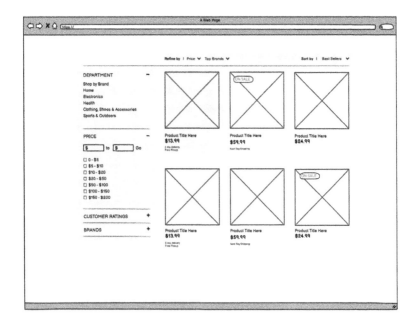

FIG 3.38: A product-browsing page template can be reused for search results and product categories.

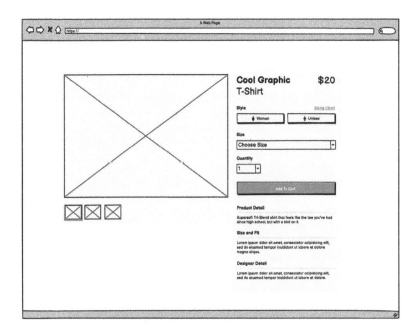

FIG 3.39: A detail page template can be reused for every product.

blog might have thousands of pages, it uses only three main templates to construct the entire website (**FIG 3.37**).

Ecommerce websites are no different. The homepage template might contain a unique set of patterns designed to entice shopping. The product-browsing and search-results pages likely share common patterns and could use the same template (**FIG 3.38**), and each product detail page typically uses one template (**FIG 3.39**).

We suggest wireframing your page templates last because they're the most time-consuming to create and working on them from scratch can be overwhelming. It's better to let your templates emerge from the process of mixing and matching the patterns you've created. Once you've wireframed a number of ideas for entire pages, you may see some similarities between them. This is a sign that you can consolidate them into a single template.

Design the fewest number of templates needed. The more unique page layouts you have, the more a user will have to learn how to use them. Much like patterns, using common templates will save time in development and make products feel familiar to your users. You don't need to develop them from scratch. Just look at the wireframes you've already made and try to identify repeating structures and patterns within them.

TAKING SHAPE

Hey, check you out! You've essentially just learned a whole new vocabulary that gives you the ability to wireframe possible solutions for your users. Learning how to use the right controls and patterns is a critical step in the path toward designing great user interfaces.

The next step has to do with understanding how humans perceive and process information, and how you can learn how to take advantage of it to optimize your wireframes. Get ready for a brief but intensive course in cognitive science and visual design!

DESIGN PRINCIPLES FOR WIREFRAMES

HAVE YOU EVER HAD A GUT FEELING? This happens even as we experience digital products. Before we're even aware of it, our subconscious:

- understands the purpose of an interface,
- judges the relevance or importance of the information being presented,
- perceives a product's aesthetics and, indirectly, its usability, and
- judges its credibility.

While we can't change the fact that humans are innately quick to judge, we can facilitate the connections happening in our users' subconscious when they engage with our products.

Basic visual design principles have been developed through centuries of art, engineering, and design. These basic principles align with how people already think—most of the time subconsciously—and, when applied properly, make our designs more usable.

We're still not talking about colors, fonts, or textures. Wireframes aren't the right place for making your UI look attractive.

Instead, we'll focus on specific visual design principles that have a real effect on how the human brain processes information. Taking a pass at the look and feel of your wireframes can help bake in some basic tenets of usability that will carry through to development.

In this section, we'll cover a few principles that you can put into practice right away: *hierarchy, alignment,* and *clarity*. While there are many design principles, we picked these three because they are the easiest to internalize and apply, and they provide a lot of return on investment toward helping your users accomplish their goals efficiently.

HIERARCHY

Understanding *visual hierarchy* means learning how our brains prioritize and categorize the things we see, and how that affects human behavior when interacting with digital interfaces.

While we often hear that humans read from left to right and top to bottom (in left-to-right languages), that assumes that the visual appearance of the words is the same. We can easily change this using the principle of hierarchy (**FIG 4.1**).

Applying hierarchy in UI design refers to the deliberate use of visual properties to make elements appear more, or less, important to the viewer.

Elements of hierarchy

There are four design elements that can be used to manipulate visual hierarchy:

- **Size.** The largest elements on a screen have the most prominence, thus holding the highest position in the hierarchy. Large text or imagery are usually noticed first when positioned in the forefront. (**FIG 4.2**).
- **Color.** Color affects hierarchy mainly by its presence, or lack thereof. Highly saturated and opaque colors represent primary importance; muted and low-opacity colors represent lower priority in a hierarchy (**FIG 4.3**).

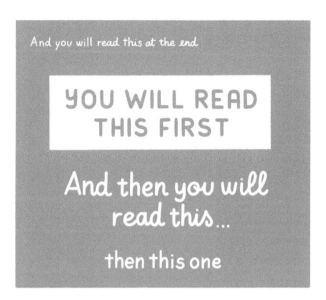

FIG 4.1: Hierarchy controls the pace of what you see and the order in which you see it.

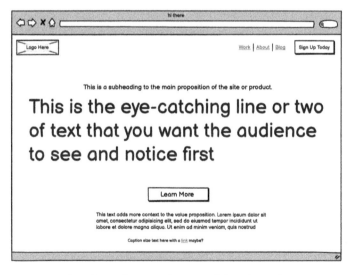

FIG 4.2: Text that is large relative to other text will draw the user's attention first, even if it doesn't appear at the top of the page.

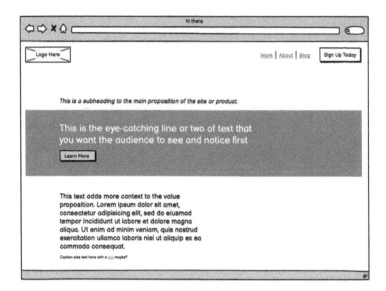

FIG 4.3: Text or other objects that have strong foreground or background colors will attract more attention than those that don't.

FIG 4.4: In cultures that read top to bottom and left to right, placing items toward the top or left sides of the screen will draw more attention than those in other locations.

FIG 4.5: UI elements that are packed densely together are harder to distinguish and, therefore, attract less attention than elements that stand alone surrounded by empty space.

- **Placement.** Elements towards the top of the page or screen are higher priority, while elements appearing on the sides or near the bottom are lower priority—particularly when scrolling is required (**FIG 4.4**).
- **White space.** Elements with more empty or negative space around them are higher in the hierarchy; elements crowded near each other compete for attention (**FIG 4.5**).

A lack of visual hierarchy interrupts the brain's ability to scan and home in on areas of interest. But clear visual hierarchy can reduce cognitive load and help users to process information more quickly and effectively (**FIG 4.6**).

If a user cannot quickly understand what they see, they become frustrated and are likely to leave the experience. UX specialist Kelley Gordon underscored this in her article, "5 Principles of Visual Design in UX":

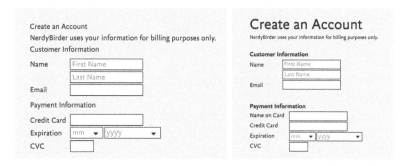

FIG 4.6: The content is the same for both forms, but the one on the right uses size and white space to create information groups that users can scan more easily.

> *Visual hierarchy controls the delivery of the experience. If you have a hard time figuring out where to look on a page, it's more than likely that its layout is missing a clear visual hierarchy. (https://bkaprt.com/wfe45/04-01)*

Since we can't control what people click on when navigating our products, we use can hierarchy as a way to suggest where they should go. Their subconscious will likely follow whatever path the hierarchy takes them on.

Understanding hierarchy

Let's look at a real-world example. Which elements of the Spotify interface command your attention first (**FIG 4.7**)?

Along with the title at the top of the screen, you probably noticed the Play button right away. That's by design. It uses size, color, and placement to stand out as the most important element in the hierarchy, even though it's not at the absolute top or side of the screen.

Scanning down to the song playlist, we see that song track names use a slightly larger font size and higher color contrast than the surrounding text (**FIG 4.8**).

While these decisions are each small on their own, they come together to create order and help our brains process the information more easily.

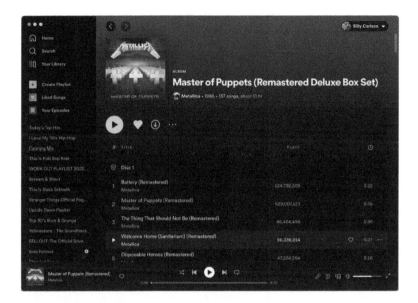

FIG 4.7: Once you learn about hierarchy, you start seeing it everywhere.

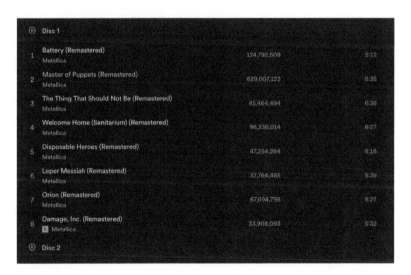

FIG 4.8: Subtle differences in color and text characteristics convey meaning that we understand subconsciously.

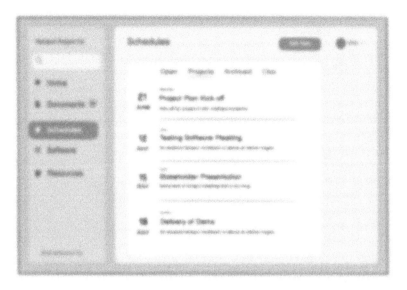

FIG 4.9: Which elements do you notice the most here?

Testing your hierarchy

What does the visual hierarchy in your wireframe say? Here are two quick and easy methods for testing the effectiveness of your hierarchy:

- **The five-second test.** This is an informal usability test, used to determine which elements stand out the most before a person has time to thoroughly analyze the design. Have someone look at the design for five seconds (you can time it!), then ask them what elements they remember from the page. Were they the most important ones? If not, you might want to change something in your visual hierarchy. Think of it as a memory test for interface design.
- **The blur test.** This test is conducted by intentionally blurring out the design's content so much that only vague shapes and colors are visible (**FIG 4.9**). Have someone look at a blurred image of the design and ask them to identify the most important areas on the page. (You can also do this

yourself without any preparation—just take a step back from the image and blur your vision by squinting. This version is aptly called a *squint test*.) If the easiest parts to see aren't also the most important, change something in your visual hierarchy.

Using hierarchy in your wireframes and UI design is a powerful way to direct attention by taking advantage of the way we naturally process information. It's a principle that is easily internalized. Apply it just a few times and soon it will become second nature.

ALIGNMENT

Alignment provides visual balance and symmetry to a layout. When done well, alignment generally goes unnoticed; only when elements are misaligned does it become distracting.

Proper alignment results in better *scannability*. Users often scan content when they first view a screen. An easy-to-scan layout guides the user's eye through high-level cues and supports them in choosing where they want to focus their attention.

Using alignment

Effectively aligning elements means paying attention to vertical and horizontal alignment within patterns and at the page level. There are a few key rules to improving alignment:

- **Align centered blocks of text along the top.** This makes it easier to allow scanning across a screen to take in each section separately (**FIG 4.10**).
- **Align large blocks of text to the left.** Blocks of text longer than three lines are easier to read when left aligned (**FIG 4.11**).
- **Align objects at the edges of the screen.** Use consistent margins on both sides of the page and align objects on the edges to them. Center alignment can visually join different elements together, such as images, text, and links (**FIG 4.12**).

FIG 4.10: Column body text that is misaligned beneath headings across the page (left) is harder to scan than text that is aligned (right).

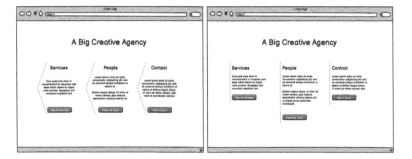

FIG 4.11: Elements that don't share a common left edge down the page are harder to scan (left) than those that do (right).

Testing your alignment

One of the easiest ways to look for alignment issues in your wireframes is to draw vertical lines down your wireframe at the start of each text element, and at the start and end of every other element (**FIG 4.13**). Then look for ways that you can adjust the edges of elements to reduce the overall number of lines (**FIG 4.14**).

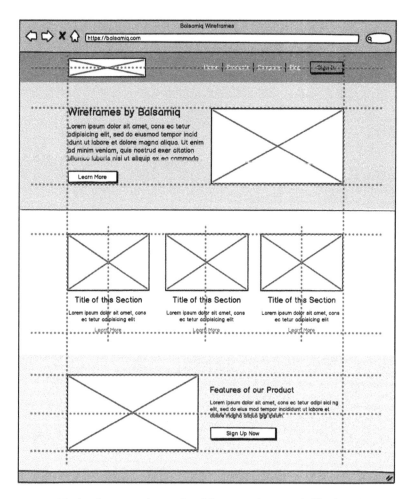

FIG 4.12: Aligning elements to the margins of the page makes pages feel less busy. Center alignment can be used to group short text with other components.

One exception to these rules is when you *want* a certain element to stand out, in which case you might not align it with others. For example, if you have a critical area that you want your users' attention to land or linger on, such as an error message (**FIG 4.15**).

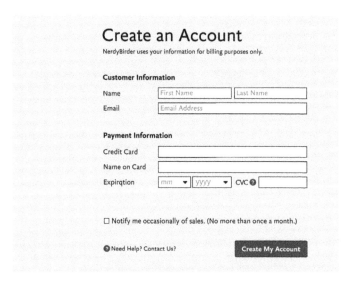

Create an Account

NerdyBirder uses your information for billing purposes only.

Customer Information

Name — First Name / Last Name

Email

Payment Information

Credit Card

Expiration — mm ▼ / yyyy ▼

CVC

☐ Notify me occasionally of sales. (No more than once a month.)

Create My Account

❓ Need Help? Contact Us?

4.13: While this wireframe does a good job with left alignment, the red lines show how misaligned a lot of the right edges are.

Create an Account

NerdyBirder uses your information for billing purposes only.

Customer Information

Name — First Name / Last Name

Email — Email Address

Payment Information

Credit Card

Name on Card

Expirqtion — mm ▼ / yyyy ▼ — CVC ❓

☐ Notify me occasionally of sales. (No more than once a month.)

❓ Need Help? Contact Us? — **Create My Account**

4.14: Consolidating shorter fields into a single row and making the longer fields all the same length creates much better alignment along the edges.

Sign Up

Business Name

A Big Creative Agency

Your Name

Billy Carlson

Your Email

billy@balsamiq.com

Your Username

BigCreative   Sorry, that username is taken

Password

Confirm Password

By signing up you are agreeing to the
Terms and Conditions and Privacy Policy

SIGN UP

FIG 4.15: Error messages attract immediate attention when they're out of alignment.

Alignment may seem subtle, but this subtlety helps make the user's path effortless and effective. These small details add up to designs that look as though they were crafted with care and not simply thrown together. Alignment demonstrates thoughtfulness and respect for the end user.

CLARITY

Clarity is less straightforward than hierarchy and alignment but is worth learning because of its impact. We like the definition of clarity that Jenifer Tidwell provides in *Designing Interfaces*: "How well the design communicates the information the designer is trying to convey." This teaches us to think about not only the message our interface sends, but what messages the user receives.

Clarity means clearing a path for your user so that they can focus on what they need to learn or do. This could mean removing roadblocks and distractions to simplify a task or adding additional text to better explain a concept. Clarity boosts the signal while reducing the noise, allowing users to find what they're looking for, to understand the options available to them, and to anticipate what will happen next when they perform an action.

This principle could also be summarized as "don't make me think," which is, of course, the title of a classic book about usability. In the book, author Steve Krug wrote that the most usable products are "self-evident," or, if that's too ambitious, "self-explanatory." Keep this in mind when you think about improving clarity.

Types of clarity

In design, clarity refers to:

- **Structure.** Use recognizable, repeated patterns and templates that are most appropriate for the content and context.
- **Content.** Ensure that you only show what's essential to get the job done. When you remove extraneous copy, images, icons, or controls that take attention away from the core of the experience, your content gains clarity.
- **Action.** Make the most important or frequent action the most prominent. A great example of clarity of action is when there is only one call to action per page (e.g., "Save," "Next," or "Buy").

At this point, we suggest that you add some real or sample content into your wireframes, especially in scenarios where content is critical to success. At minimum, you can try to think about the number of words in your interface and whether you can remove some. You can also review the spacing and hierarchy in your wireframes to better guide users through each screen.

FIG 4.16: When you have a lot of information on one page it can become overwhelming (left). Consider collapsing the details and showing only the most important pieces of information (right).

Using clarity

You can enhance clarity by grouping, hiding, or removing elements:

- **Grouping:** When you look at your design, take a few extra moments to see if you can group any elements together (e.g., form fields that are part of a whole, like an address).
- **Hiding:** Evaluate the priority of what's on the screen, using subject matter expertise when appropriate. Identify elements that might be optional, or even rarely used, and consider hiding them using a dropdown, accordion, or other method for condensing content (**FIG 4.16**).

- **Removing:** As you go through this process, some elements will lose importance. It might sound harsh, but ask yourself whether they need to be there at all. You can improve clarity and provide a better experience by only showing what's essential.

Each project is different, and the approach to designing for clarity varies, based on users and their needs. For example, if you're creating an application for an ordering kiosk at a restaurant, you can provide clarity through your use of unambiguous wording, appropriate selection controls, and obvious buttons. However, if you're creating the next big video sharing app, you'll create clarity by prioritizing a few key actions and minimizing other content so that the user doesn't get distracted. Clarity always supports users in achieving their goals.

JUST ENOUGH DESIGN

The design principles described in this chapter may, at first, seem inconsequential or even subjective, when applied to a single interface element or pattern. But when you apply them consistently across your wireframes, they function as a subconscious instruction manual for using your product that carries over to development. If you've applied these principles deliberately to your wireframes, you and your team increase the likelihood of delivering a highly usable product.

So now let's learn how to incorporate your team into the process. You've come too far to just toss your wireframes over the wall and hope for the best. To get the best solution in front of customers, you'll need to work with every role on your team and learn how to wireframe together. Don't worry, we've got a process for that too!

WIREFRAMING
AS A TEAM

WHEN ONE OF THE AUTHORS of this book interviewed for his first design job, the design team showed him their gorgeous design library. Accessible through a centralized intranet, it contained the guidelines and resources they had created for the company's various products.

But when he started the job, he was surprised to find that, aside from a few recognizable icons and logos, none of the design team's work was reflected in the actual products. He soon learned that his new colleagues provided pixel-perfect screen designs to the software engineering team, but the designs rarely made it to production.

Since he was new and in his first job, he didn't feel comfortable questioning the process. He and the other designers communicated with the software engineers exclusively via email, even though their team was just on the other side of the building. In his first six months, he rarely left the corner of the office where the design team sat. He only talked to other designers, and they spent most of their conversations complaining about the engineering team.

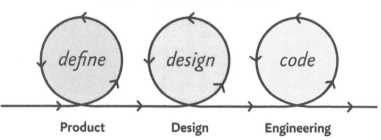

The Product Triad

define   design   code

Product   Design   Engineering

FIG 5.1: The product triad is a common framework in many organizations that includes business, design, and engineering roles.

It didn't matter how good the team's design work was, or what tools they used to create the designs. The company didn't have a collaborative culture. They all worked on the same product, but they weren't on the same team.

DESIGN IN THE REAL WORLD

If you work within a software department, even outside of the technology industry, your site or application will probably pass through three standard general phases—problem definition, design, and coding—with separate groups or departments leading each one. This division of responsibilities is sometimes called the *product triad* (**FIG 5.1**).

In a typical product triad configuration, a product owner (who may have a title such as product manager, business analyst, or even CEO) usually leads or is heavily involved in the definition phase, often producing requirements or specification documents. One or more UX or UI designers are responsible for the design phase, where they will create wireframes and/or prototypes. And software engineers (a.k.a. developers) write code that is then tested before releasing the product to customers.

The product triad is effective because it employs the range and depth of specialized skills needed to make a successful

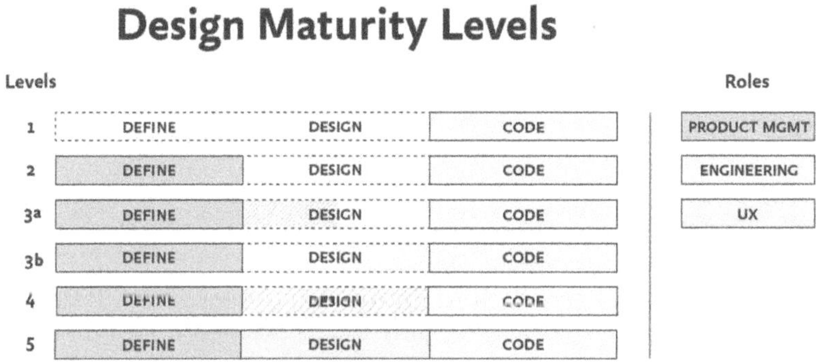

Design Maturity Levels

Levels				Roles
1	DEFINE	DESIGN	CODE	PRODUCT MGMT
2	DEFINE	DESIGN	CODE	ENGINEERING
3a	DEFINE	DESIGN	CODE	UX
3b	DEFINE	DESIGN	CODE	
4	DEFINE	DESIGN	CODE	
5	DEFINE	DESIGN	CODE	

FIG 5.2: The five levels of design maturity in organizations, as visualized by Dan Olsen (https://bkaprt.com/wfe45/05-01). Levels 1-4 have a "design gap," where a dedicated UX role is absent.

product. But it also leads to silos, which inhibit communication and collaboration across areas, leading to stories like the one above. This challenge gets compounded when the design phase is perfunctory or abbreviated, which is not uncommon, even today.

In his experience as a product consultant, Dan Olsen, author of *The Lean Product Playbook*, observed that many software organizations don't even have a dedicated designer for every project, resulting in a "design gap" that product and engineering roles attempt to fill. He created a diagram to visualize the types of configurations he sees, according to five levels of design maturity (FIG 5.2).

In Olsen's view, organizations at Levels 1 and 2 don't practice intentional design and the product team is focused on functionality. Level 3 is when product management or engineering makes some attempt at user experience design. Level 4 is when product management and engineering collaborate on the design. And level 5 is when a UI or UX designer is finally added to bridge the gap.

We anticipate that many of the readers of this book will see themselves somewhere between levels 1 and 4. Even with a designer on staff, many teams are not fully utilizing the role of design to bridge the gap between product and engineering.

Working on a team with a UX design gap can be frustrating. It creates a situation where people are doing work they aren't practically trained to do, even if they really care about design.

There can be a positive side to this, however, because these clear gaps can encourage, or even require, people to work outside of their silos. Involving non-designers in the design process can produce ideas and possibilities unimaginable to a siloed designer. Seize this opportunity!

Many roles across an organization can collaborate around wireframes. In fact, we rarely see the exact same configuration twice. Maybe you can picture how various members of your team might use wireframes in their roles: business analysts, product managers, project managers, CEOs, marketers, content designers, backend and frontend developers, training leads, customer support specialists, UX engineers, and more. The beauty is that most people in these roles wouldn't describe themselves as designers, yet they're *designing* by contributing their voice to the design process.

WHAT TEAM WIREFRAMING LOOKS LIKE

The most effective teams reach beyond their disciplines to share responsibility for a successful process. That shared responsibility is a critical component of teams that wireframe together, whether they have designated design roles or not.

Picture a relay race: on each competing team, four athletes take turns running consecutive sprints around the track, aiming to get their last runner across the finish line the fastest. In addition to running as fast as they can during their sprint, each runner must hand a baton swiftly and securely to the next runner (FIG 5.3).

If a runner drops the baton or doesn't negotiate the transfer smoothly, the runners' speed won't matter—the race is over. Winning teams need fast runners *and* skilled handoffs.

See where we're going here?

Shipping great digital products relies on individuals who produce great work and support smooth, collaborative handoffs

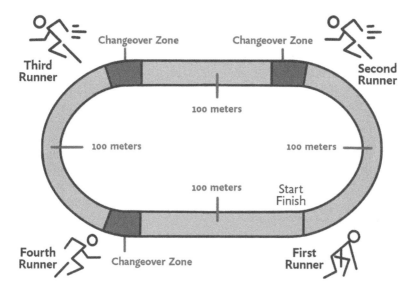

FIG 5.3: The best software teams take responsibility for receiving and transferring the baton to their teammates.

of their work between roles. Moreover, you can't ship great products if you concentrate solely on your part of the project. An individual's contribution may help or hurt a team, but it's how the team performs collectively that leads to success (or failure).

Any design process that values communication and collaboration over deliverables relies on the handoff between critical roles. And, just like on a relay race team, training for the handoff (passing the baton) is just as important as producing the work (running a lap).

So, where does wireframing fit in all of this? Wireframes are great for teams because they support the work happening *within* each of these phases and the necessary transitions *between* them.

PRINCIPLES OF TEAM WIREFRAMING

Wireframes don't add value to the product—customers don't buy, install, or use wireframes. Their value is that the action of wireframing itself adds to the design process. Teams that wireframe together can improve their internal communication and collaboration while shipping a better product.

Wireframing is more than just creating artifacts; it's a process of collaborative design. The most essential ingredient in this process is the people—more specifically, how those people communicate and cooperate. It's important to start with some basic principles for how you'll use wireframes as a team. Here are our suggestions.

Be explicit about handoffs

Treat handoffs with care. They are critical points in the process. Don't make assumptions about what the next person will expect from or do with incoming artifacts. With communication as a core component, several techniques contribute to successful handoffs:

- **Document the existing handoff process.** Spend time up front creating an inventory of the various artifacts you're using and the types of communication between steps. And, make note of *when* each type of communication happens. You'll be able to view your current workflow as a team and identify gaps or opportunities for improvement.
- **Allow each team member to describe what they need to fulfill their role.** Let each person in a role explain what information is most important to them and in what form they prefer it, such as wireframes, sample data, or performance criteria. People are rarely asked these questions, and it can be enlightening for the rest of the team to hear their answers. Teammates often make false assumptions based on their own preferences.
- **Reframe each person's role to include responsibility for the handoff.** If you have a step-by-step process, make sure that the transition steps are part of it. It should be clear to

everyone that their job isn't done until the next person has everything they need.

Once you've completed the handoff, stay informed about other roles' work. Fortunately, most modern software tools offer collaboration features. Many wireframing tools support real-time viewing, editing, and commenting for multiple users (similar to Google Docs), or the ability to mention users or groups by name and determine how and when they're notified (as in Slack).

People who are actively participating in the handoff might want a notification for every change or comment, while others who are further upstream or downstream may just want to subscribe to a digest or summary of updates as a way of keeping up asynchronously.

If you're handling multiple phases of the project yourself (e.g., both product management and design), it's still valuable to work through each phase as though there's a handoff happening between them. Each phase has separate goals and deliverables, after all.

Know your goals

In Chapter 1, we identified what wireframes look like at different stages of the design process—early, middle, and late. But in a team context, it's also crucial to think about what you're using the wireframes for at each stage.

Wireframes fulfill a variety of purposes throughout the process:

1. **Articulation.** Early in the process, use wireframes to represent a clear visualization of the problem, one that's easy to reference throughout the design process. It's critical to identify and articulate the problem and its current state so that you can avoid wasting time exploring casual assumptions.
2. **Generation.** Wireframes can stimulate and facilitate creativity. By nature, they're unrefined and offer the right amount of constraint so that you can rapidly create many varied ideas without judgment or getting stuck in tunnel vision.

3. **Iteration.** Since you can easily edit and revise them, wireframes are invaluable for building and improving upon early ideas, as well as throughout the product lifecycle. Planning and creating opportunity for input and involvement beyond the initial design phase yields better solutions and prevents problems in later phases. Productive iteration means that you can remove unnecessary or infeasible ideas to deliver a *minimum viable product* (MVP) or get to market sooner.

4. **Communication.** You can present wireframes to stakeholders or clients to focus attention on structural elements like workflow and layout, which are difficult or even impossible to change later in the process—as opposed to decisions about fonts, colors, and other details that may evolve with the design. Developers can use wireframes as implementation guides, providing an overview as well as detailed views and annotations for technical specs like CSS properties or animation parameters.

5. **Validation.** Share wireframes with customers for user testing and with engineering teams for quality assurance or technical review, before coding starts or gets too far along. Using wireframes to validate design ideas will help you catch anything you might have missed before moving on to code.

Whenever you wireframe, be clear about your goals, and communicate those goals to anyone you share the wireframe with.

Annotate your wireframes

Regardless of your role, there may be aspects of your ideas that are hard to communicate through a user interface wireframe alone. That's why *annotations*—non-UI elements such as notes, arrows, and callouts like you might draw on a whiteboard (**FIG 5.4**)—are so helpful, because they can easily explain what's hard to show.

There are many ways of annotating and many reasons for using them. In an article called "Design annotations that will make your developers happy," designer Grace Noh offered advice about what and when to annotate your wireframes

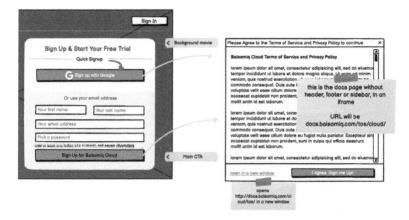

FIG 5.4: An annotation is anything in your wireframe that doesn't represent part of the user interface. They often have distinctive styles or colors so that they don't get mistaken for part of the interface.

(https://bkaprt.com/wfe45/05-02). She cited four scenarios where annotations are especially effective:

Showing error and edge cases
1. *Describing off-screen experiences*
2. *Sharing design rationale*
3. *Tracking changes and decisions*

For example, you could add annotations to identify the steps that happen in the background when a user clicks or taps a button, rather than building out additional screens for every step. You might use annotations to explain why you've included certain form fields, or to ask your teammates clarifying questions about various aspects of the design.

Annotations can be especially useful when handing off to developers, who may need to know about animations and other dynamic interactions that involve movement or occur over time. While it might feel like a fun challenge to try to wireframe these interactions, it could be faster and more effective to design only one state and describe the remaining states in words. And if another part of your product functions similarly, write a note

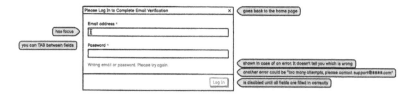

FIG 5.5: Placing annotations next to the parts of the wireframe they refer to makes them more immediate, but potentially cluttered if there are too many of them.

FIG 5.6: Using numbered callouts makes the interface less cluttered but is more work to review the notes associated with them.

to indicate that, rather than trying to recreate it; the developer might be able to reuse the same code. Win-win.

You can place annotations directly on or adjacent to the area they relate to (**FIG 5.5**), or they can take the form of callouts (**FIG 5.6**), where numbered indicators are placed on the UI and the comments are in a separate area of the screen or even a different panel of the application.

When adding annotations, try to think how other team members will interpret them. Include answers to the questions you anticipate. Draw attention to areas that you want to emphasize or call attention to. Soon, you'll get a feel for the right level and type of information that your team finds useful.

WIREFRAMING ROLES AND RESPONSIBILITIES

Because wireframes are quick and easy to create and understand, and don't require any prerequisite skills to make, they can facilitate handoffs between roles across all process phases. Work to get everyone on your team comfortable with using and receiving wireframes as you incorporate them into your process.

Not all digital product teams are familiar with the concept of shared responsibility, so you need to define who does what—specifically for your team. Too much ownership by one role or team can result in silos, while not enough can create apathy or indifference. The key to finding the right balance is having some degree of overlap between steps in the process, regardless of where the handoffs occur.

The product role

A product manager (PM) is responsible for getting the project off to a good start by defining the problem and providing the designer with resources. Good product managers will pass along documents or user stories, but great product managers can use wireframes to visualize, clarify, and communicate ideas.

As a PM, you can use wireframes to explore and present rough ideas or high-level views of key screens or steps in the workflow. While you may have a deep understanding of the problem, try to avoid prescribing a specific solution early on, so that a wider range of possibilities may emerge.

Your wireframes shouldn't look like a completed design. Use basic shapes and annotations to show customer flows or conditional behaviors, or make a wireflow (as described in Chapter 2) to show connections between screens.

It's common (and easy!) for people to add too many details to wireframes, but it's important that you include only the most meaningful elements. When in doubt, focus on articulating the problem by visualizing pain points, showing the current workflow, or sketching out rough ideas with plenty of annotations to clarify your thinking.

The design role

If you're used to being the go-to UI person, working in a wire-frame-centered process can be challenging. If you're a designer (or take on that role as *de facto* designer), you may expect to create and deliver *the* design. But embracing wireframing as a team means that, in most cases, you're making wireframes for the purpose of delivering information rather than creating an archival representation of the final product.

The designer's main job in the wireframing process is to produce as many ideas as possible and show them to others for refinement and iteration. Applying your knowledge of UI patterns and UX best practices will allow you to create possibilities that help move the design conversation forward. People in other roles on the team will become much more engaged through giving feedback on your designs than having to generate solutions on their own.

A designer's second biggest task is to ask questions. Aim to get everything relevant out of the PM's head and onto the screen, so ask questions like:

- What percentage of users will use this feature?
- How do they accomplish this task now?
- Does the user have to make this choice? Can we automate or expedite the choice selection?
- What is the user's goal on this screen?
- Where would users expect to find this link/function/etc.?

This may mean that you create deliberately incomplete wire-frames. It may mean that you share multiple concepts with the intention of getting critical feedback, rather than showing off your work in order to get approval. It most certainly means creating a lot of wireframes that you wouldn't share on Dribbble or any other design showcase website.

Wireframes don't need to be pretty to be effective. As designer Shipra Kayan elegantly stated in her article, "Align Your Team Around Customer Needs via Design Workshops," "Try not to be 'the designer.' Instead, focus on creating space for other people to have insights, ideate, and design" (https:// bkaprt.com/wfe45/05-03).

As a designer, you perform the middle step in the process, meaning that you accept information from the PM *and* deliver information to development. You should go back and forth between them. While it may be demanding, your role has the benefit of inhabiting multiple worlds and speaking multiple languages. You're part shepherd, part translator.

Get into the habit of delivering *at least three rounds* of wireframes. The first round comes after you have clarified the requirements with the PM, another after getting feedback from the PM, and at least one more once you've shown the updated wireframes to the developer.

It's important that the developer sees any wireframes you and the PM have created, and that the PM has a chance to learn from their feedback. The developer may provide new information based on what they're viewing, such as time estimates or technical constraints, which could influence the PM's decision to pursue the complete design. If there is disagreement or pushback, you can get back on track by asking them what's most important.

The development role

Developers often use wireframes to make communication with other roles easier. The language of programming can be obscure and unfamiliar to those who aren't immersed in it.

Working with wireframes ensures that everyone is talking about the same thing when discussing the UI design. Wireframes provide common ground when words might be insufficient or misunderstood. They come together to act as a map that aligns visual elements and words, similar to how universal iconography helps people who don't speak the same language (FIG 5.7).

One of the most useful things you can communicate to the designer is what will be easy and what will be difficult to code. Get comfortable with reviewing and providing feedback on design wireframes. You might also add annotations, or design workflows for stress cases.

FIG 5.7: Airports use icons and other visuals for shared understanding despite language barriers. (Photograph courtesy of Laura Farolfi)

FIG 5.8: Wireframes help you get a technical idea out of your head and onto the screen.

As a developer, you can use wireframes to help visualize, illustrate, share, and discuss your ideas, similar to how a PM might share theirs. But, unlike a PM, your wireframes might visualize technical concepts, such as database queries (FIG 5.8).

Also, think about design solutions that are better from an engineering perspective that might accomplish the same result or solve the same problem. It could be worth the trade-off to implement a slightly less ideal solution for the user if it is much faster, safer, or more useful from a technical perspective.

If abstract wireframing feels too disconnected from code, try creating a basic library of wireframe components (or work with a designer if you have one) that map to your pattern library or design system (FIG 5.9). Then you can use those wireframe components to represent real code components. You don't need to use precise color values or font sizes because those are already defined in your coding framework or style sheet, but you can start to assemble UI screens or dialogs as if they were Lego bricks (FIG 5.10).

Title Text

Second Level Text

Selected object

Default object

Default text

Default Button

Primary Button

FIG 5.9: You can create a wireframe or guide to show the mapping of wireframe elements to real application or web components.

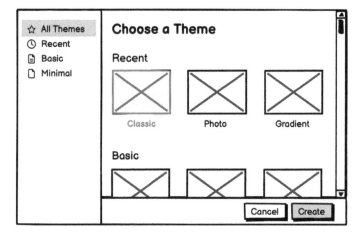

FIG 5.10: A wireframe based on a collection of code library components.

If you're filling in a design gap or acting as a designer, try to distance yourself from the lens of technology frameworks and technical limitations when you're wireframing. It doesn't mean that those considerations are irrelevant, but they may limit your imagination. Try looking at other products for inspiration, as it may help to step out of your role as a technical insider.

Wireframes are a great tool for designing effective products, but the tool itself isn't the only element necessary for success. A group of experienced cooks using dull knives can make a better meal than inexperienced cooks using sharp knives. Knowing—and trusting—who does what and when, and how to use available tools, is key.

FACING CHALLENGES AS A TEAM

Whatever your team's configuration, you'll learn one another's strengths and weaknesses as you come together to collaborate.

As you start to incorporate wireframing into your process, don't worry if things don't go perfectly. When conflict does arise—and this is a *when*, not an *if*—here are a few tips for working through challenges.

Revisit the problem

Companies that are driven by sales teams or focused on rapid growth often add features aggressively without reflecting on the problem they're solving. Continually adding everything customers ask for leads to a product that fewer customers want because it becomes too complex, suffers from poor performance, or is too expensive.

A good product owner must be willing to make tough choices, see the tradeoffs, and say no to some requests. Sometimes just asking, "What's the problem we're trying to solve?" can reframe things enough to generate better ideas.

Explain your decisions

A lot of people in non-design roles have had negative experiences with know-it-all designers who deliver attractive, polished designs without any rationale or justification. As a result, it's not unusual for others to feel intimidated by or skeptical of the role of design. A good designer should be able to explain their design decisions, so don't be afraid to ask.

When presenting designs, include your rationale to back up your design decisions. Share your research, or even conduct some usability studies to show how real people encounter the challenges you're trying to solve.

Seek first to understand

It can take a soft touch—and time—to build trust. Start by taking the time to learn things outside of your area of expertise. Designers can try to understand what makes development hard. Developers can listen to users more. Everyone should understand who the customer is and what they care about.

At the same time, don't assume that you and those outside of your role don't care about the same things. There are plenty of developers who are passionate about UX, and designers who want to better understand technology.

Most problems boil down to misunderstanding, not malice, which means you probably have more control over conflicts than you imagine. Improving communication involves a lot of people, so if someone next to you isn't happy with what they're getting, think about how and what you're communicating, and what you can do differently. Win the whole relay race, not just your leg.

Build connection

When we interviewed designer Emileigh Barnes, she told us that her two go-to strategies for building relationships with colleagues are asking for help and sharing experiences (https:// bkaprt.com/wfe45/05-04). Make an effort to build trust and camaraderie with teammates. Suggest going out (or meeting virtually) for coffee or lunch. Look for opportunities to participate in facilitated team-building activities, or attend a talk or conference together. Start by asking questions. It might take pushing yourself outside of your comfort zone, but it can lead to a more connected team.

WIREFRAMING BETTER TOGETHER

Wireframes are a powerful tool for teams because they're approachable and collaborative. They allow everyone to participate in product design, rather than depending on one person with highly specialized skills. Wireframes democratize the design process and invite diverse perspectives and skillsets—contributing to more accessible, humane products.

The process of wireframing serves as a foundation for building a team culture of mutual support and shared success. By using this process, you unlock opportunities for communication that can expand across disciplines, encouraging every teammate to contribute.

With a clear view of the problem you're trying to solve and a unified team spirit, you can move beyond simply visualizing the final product to fundamentally changing it through the use of wireframes. So now that your team is on the same page, you're ready to start sharing and improving them together.

6

ESTABLISHING A FEEDBACK PROCESS

ARTIST AND EDUCATOR SISTER CORITA KENT kept ten rules for herself and her students posted on her studio walls in the Immaculate Heart College art department (https://bkaprt.com/wfe45/06-01). Rule number eight was:

> Don't try to create and analyze at the same time. They're different processes.

The two sentences sound deceptively simple, don't they? The sentiment may even seem obvious, but let's unpack this a bit to see how powerful it can be for thinking about design feedback. Notice the key words:

- To *create* is to put together.
- To *analyze* is to take apart.

Each activity requires a different frame of mind; doing them simultaneously can be counterproductive. That's why we wait to analyze until after we've created—and analysis is its own art form. It's also why we've waited this long to introduce it; it's better, and easier, to analyze after you've spent ample time in the creation mindset.

Designing a product should be a collaborative effort where you can count on feedback to push the process forward. Reviewing your ideas while still in the wireframing phase is a great way to collect feedback and iterate on your designs quickly, effectively, and flexibly.

It's tempting to jump into redesigning the moment you receive feedback, but wait a bit. The next round of creative activity will come *after* you've had time to reflect on what you've learned and thought about what to do to make the solution more effective—after you're out of analysis mode. Follow a process to make the most of the time you spend reviewing.

Design critique is a practice that we've used repeatedly to elicit useful feedback on our wireframes. It's a process used in all types of creative practices, from graphic design to film, to user experience—based around the intent to evaluate ideas against defined criteria at various stages of completion. Critiques are typically organized as a facilitated discussion of the proposed design and analysis of how it meets objectives. Your goal is to get enough information to improve the design.

CONSTRUCTIVE FEEDBACK

When design critiques go well, you'll be surprised by the quantity and quality of helpful insights you collect for evolving your design. Over time, you'll likely start seeking others' input earlier and more often as you understand its value. But successful feedback sessions rarely happen by accident; they result from purpose and intention.

Facilitating a design critique can sometimes feel like a bombardment of judgment and criticism. A better way to approach these sessions is to remember that your wireframes are supposed to serve users and their goals. Approach it with a sense of objectivity and detachment.

Effective analysis and evaluation should be *constructive*, not *destructive*. It's an evolutionary act meant to improve product design in future iterations. The goal is to use analysis to spur the next creative pass.

But how do you know when feedback is constructive, or even useful? In their book *Discussing Design* (https://bkaprt.com/wfe45/06-02), Adam Connor and Aaron Irizarry provide a few characteristics of useful feedback, which we've expanded on below.

Constructive feedback in the design process is:

- **Based in trust.** The people providing and receiving feedback must trust each other. Feedback discussions start with a common goal and expectation: to find ways to improve the product as a team.
- **Analytical.** Good feedback encourages critical thinking. As you break down the wireframe into parts, analyze how each element contributes to the solution as a whole. Point out what you see in a wireframe and state why it might prevent a user from completing a task. For instance, instead of calling the navigation options "confusing," an analytical observation might sound like this: "The navigation hides the path to settings that we think the user may be looking for, like privacy preferences."
- **Clear and specific.** Good feedback describes the problem using clear language. Try to hone in on details, such as "The word 'cancel' could be misinterpreted by users as canceling their subscription instead of canceling the changes they made to their account." This is clearer than saying only "the button is confusing," which could refer to the button's behavior, placement, label, or other characteristics.
- **Open-ended.** Good feedback avoids offering solutions. This allows the designer to develop new ideas and gives them time to explore solutions more fully than they might achieve by responding to off-the-cuff proposals in the moment.
- **Objective.** Good feedback focuses on project goals and user needs, rather than on personal feelings. Assess whether the design helps users achieve their goals. For example, an evaluative observation might sound like this: "The call-to-action button is not very prominent in the design. If that button is

meant to lead to a primary goal when viewing this screen, the user might miss it."

- **Actionable**. Good feedback is practical and can be used for improving the design. For example, in critiquing an address form, you might say that users in other countries would be confused—but it won't be as useful as providing specific suggestions for the field labels, for example. Here's an actionable observation: "This form's design makes it difficult for users outside the United States to understand how to enter information. Consider localizing the labelling, so that the fields reflect what's relevant for each country."

Despite knowing what makes feedback useful, you'll undoubtedly run into ineffective and even unusable feedback from time to time. Knowing how to identify and respond to counterproductive feedback is part of creating a productive feedback cycle. In *Discussing Design,* the authors note that *counterproductive* feedback is often:

- **Reactive.** Reactive feedback provides a purely emotional reaction without analysis. Reactive feedback may sound like an emotional or gut response, such as, "I hate this idea," or, "I love what you've done there!" Personal opinions *rarely* reflect your user's opinions.
- **Directional**. Directional feedback provides alternative solutions rather than sharing an evaluation of the design. Solution-based input may sound like, "I would do this differently," or, "let's put this in the settings page instead." It reflects personal bias or a conclusion articulated without context. Suggestions are okay, but always provide them with a reason why, starting with why the current proposal isn't ideal.

Don't dismiss counterproductive feedback outright, however. Get curious, dig a little deeper, and ask clarifying questions like, "What do you mean by that?" or, "How does this solve our user's problem?" Ideally, answers to these questions will provide clearer, more usable feedback.

Learn how to receive feedback

To meaningfully receive feedback, you have to listen and reflect. The practice of *active listening* can be very helpful here. This allows reviewers to feel heard while helping receivers hear more attentively by reflecting back to the reviewer what they've heard. The feedback-giver is responsible for confirming or clarifying feedback until they feel they've been heard.

The practice comes from the field of psychology and is used by counselors to give people a repeatable model for sympathetically communicating with their partners. Because the listener must reflect back what they've heard, they learn to stay engaged in listening and understanding, rather than in preparing how they will respond.

So why do we do this in a design critique? It helps participants better understand what the presenter is sharing, and it encourages them to express themselves clearly. The exchange might require a few attempts for both parties to successfully communicate. That's normal.

Expressing thoughts may not come easily for everyone. Some have a hard time getting to the point, while others don't know what they're trying to say until they explore their thoughts out loud. The back-and-forth exercise of speaking and reflecting really helps in this regard.

Learn how to give feedback

If you're able to conduct feedback sessions as part of your regular process, everyone will soon find themselves as a reviewer. For this role, consider having a checklist of things for reviewers to keep in mind. As reviewers looks at each wireframe, they should ask themselves if the solution helps the user perform their task or accomplish their goal.

When it's your turn to give feedback, you might start by asking questions that help you understand why the presenter executed their idea as they did, such as:

- Why did you decide to use this type of X (e.g., interaction, component, design pattern)?

- How does this idea align with the user's intent in this scenario?
- What are some other ideas we could explore that might also be effective?
- What (if anything) isn't feasible?
- Does this solve the right problem?

You should also look closely at the details of the design—interface components used, interactions the user will have, layout of elements—to see if they help or detract from successful task completion. For instance, you might ask:

- How does this content help support the user's goal?
- Can the user understand this content?
- Does this interaction make it easy, or even possible, to complete the task?
- Does this interaction slow down or create obstacles to completing the task?
- Is anything missing in the design?

Last, don't forget that you can include positive reactions in your feedback. Positive feedback is a great motivator, and can make tougher assessments easier to swallow. It's just as important for the designer to know what's working well in their wireframe as it is to know what needs improvement.

SUCCESSFUL DESIGN CRITIQUE

Product success is often the result of numerous concept explorations, team discussions, user testing, and going back to the drawing board. This is an essential cycle because we need critique to deliver the right design. Getting it early and frequently results in shipping higher quality products.

Running successful design critiques can be tricky, however. You may even encounter tension and disagreement, which is why it's important to have a process for reviewing and discussing wireframes. You will need to decide who to involve, how to ask for productive feedback, and most importantly how to facilitate discussion. The outcome of successful feedback sessions will provide actionable information for design iterations.

Determine what (and when) to critique

As you gain experience in creating wireframes, you'll start to develop a sense of when your idea needs feedback—like when you've explored an idea enough that it seems to represent the project requirements. Request feedback when you're ready to:

- Discuss initial concepts for further clarification and exploration
- Find the most effective solution among many concepts
- Analyze a design (or a discrete portion) for improvement
- Evaluate concepts against usability heuristics and design principles (the next chapter on optimizing for usability will touch on these)

This isn't an exact science; there are all sorts of situations where you'll feel ready to share. When you've taken your idea as far as it can go on your own, that's a great indicator to ask for input. Trust your gut. The more you do it, the easier it will be to tune into feeling ready.

The types of feedback you'll get will vary at different stages. During the early stage of wireframes, feedback sessions might be quick and will spur immediate changes. Expect frequent feedback because initial concepts often head in the wrong direction. You might go back to the drawing board repeatedly at the beginning of a project. Whereas, later in the process, you will have added more information to your design. At these later stages, you'll inspect the details.

At a minimum, ask for feedback at two points in your design process: once when you're about thirty percent done, and once at around ninety percent. The Thirty Percent Feedback approach comes 42Floors' Jason Freedman, inspired by their investor, Seth Lieberman, who encouraged regular early feedback before big changes became too laborious (https://bkaprt. com/wfe45/06-03). The idea is to request "thirty percent feedback" in the early stages, with the shared understanding that the presenter won't have all the details finalized and the reviewer will focus their attention on high-level issues. When you think that your wireframe is nearly complete, you can request "ninety percent feedback"—minimal big changes, but focusing on adjusting and correcting the tiny details.

You can encourage the right kind of feedback at the thirty percent and ninety percent stages by being deliberate about the fidelity of your wireframes (as we explained in Chapter 1). The feedback level you receive should correspond to the level of fidelity of your wireframes. High-level (low-fidelity) sketches will result in high-level feedback; detailed (high-fidelity) wireframes should net more detailed input.

There is no hard and fast rule here about when to ask for feedback. With practice and experience you'll know when the design is ready. Start by encouraging early feedback reviews, because it's the hardest—due to fear of showing unfinished work—and sets a precedent for the rest of the design process.

Decide who to involve

Carefully consider whom to involve in critiques. Only include those who are integral to moving the project forward at that stage and whose opinions matter most.

Your core group can include:

- **Team members.** These people will likely fill a wide range of roles, from product managers and developers to user researchers and other interface designers. They will help with decision-making and advocate for the user and the product, objectively using your feedback framework. Regardless of role, your teammates can also jump in to serve as note-takers and observers.
- **Subject matter experts.** These people have product relevant knowledge and can contribute useful input toward the success of your project. For instance, if you're working on an app for stock trading, you'll need experts who are familiar with order flow and legal issues that will influence what goes into the interface. They may be outside of the core

team, but they often welcome and appreciate having their voices heard early on.

- **Stakeholders.** These are any other people who are invested in the project's success. Stakeholders might include internal product owners and leadership, as well as external clients and partners. They're accountable for final decisions on the project. In some cases, they may hold financial responsibility. In early stages, you might only want to include stakeholders who are actively involved in the work. In later stages, you may need to incorporate higher-up stakeholders to keep them informed, while some might never want to be involved in critiques at all.

Whomever you invite, expect and encourage them to be an active participant. If you don't want their opinion, don't include them. Try to discern which group members *must* be present for every critique to advance the design to the next stage.

Facilitate constructive discussion

If you've created the wireframes that you want to present for feedback, you'll likely be the critique facilitator. A discussion facilitator involves being a presenter, mediator, timekeeper, and manager all at once. We won't delve too deeply into the discipline of facilitation, though we have included some great resources in the back of the book. Just remember that your main role is to guide the conversation by:

- Establishing goals and guidelines for the discussion
- Encouraging (but not forcing) participation from everyone
- Keeping the discussion focused on analysis
- Moving the discussion forward when stuck
- Getting enough actionable information to use for iteration

It's your job to prepare the team—and yourself—for rich discussion, and undoubtedly some disagreement. In his book *Design for Cognitive Bias*, David Dylan Thomas wrote:

[...] when we elicit feedback or facilitate workshops that require different people to communicate honestly to make decisions, we need to make sure there is a valid path for dissent (https:// bkaprt.com/wfe45/06-04).

To get the discussion started, consider using a technique like Round Robin. In this technique, you go around the room (or call), giving each participant a chance to offer their feedback. This can be a useful way to include everyone in the conversation.

If you're not asking every participant for feedback in order, remember that some members of the team may be more chatty or outspoken than others. Be sure to actively solicit the feedback of quieter team members to allow for all personality types to participate.

Some participants may not be prepared to speak on the spot, may need time to reflect, or may have other reasons for not wanting to share with the group. Allow them to contribute in a different way, such as sharing their feedback afterwards in a manner that allows them to speak freely. This can add to your time, to process and share back the information, but it's a good way to make sure that you hear from everyone.

Walk through the wireframes

Before you start the discussion, the facilitator should walk through the wireframes to present the design. You can jump right in and review each screen sequentially, but we recommend starting with an overview of the features and screens first, then walking through each wireframe, especially if you're presenting a complex design with a lot of screens. We'll often discuss requirements, user flows, or user scenarios before digging into the individual wireframes.

Decide whether you want to respond to comments during the presentation or go through the entire walkthrough first and take questions afterward—and make sure the participants know which approach to use. We often work in teams where the number of participants is small enough to discuss efficiently as we go, but we've also worked with the same teammates for years, so there is a certain amount of chemistry, ease, and trust in our sessions. With a variable or new group of participants, it may make more sense to get feedback after presenting the entire design.

Frame the presentation in the user's terms—walk through the design from their perspective. You might say things like, "When the user arrives at this screen, they can do X by selecting Y." This helps focus participants on user goals as they discuss the wireframes. It also helps the participants visualize and imagine completing the tasks from the user's perspective. If you start hearing a lot of "I would do..." or "Why would I want to..." comments, try to redirect the conversation back to what the user might do or want instead, based on your research or problem statements.

Document the session

You'll need a dedicated notetaker other than the facilitator for these sessions. The facilitator must focus fully on facilitation, and they can't do that while producing a detailed account of the discussion. It's easy to miss things when you're engaged in conversation.

Establish guidelines for the notetaking, to create shared expectations for the notes and to make it easier for the notetaker to capture what's important. For each piece of feedback, ask them to note the wireframe, the relevant area of the screen, the comment or observation, and who made the comment. These details will help you later if you need to follow up and seek clarification.

There are different approaches to take to make feedback visible during the discussion. During in-person sessions, the notetaker could use sticky notes to capture issues, which you could then use to identify themes through grouping and affinity mapping. Alternatively, the notetaker could use a whiteboard, or type into a wiki page projected onto a portion of the screen. There are many digital tools for collaborative notetaking that you can use during remote feedback sessions as well.

You can even conduct asynchronous critique sessions by asking reviewers to give feedback directly on the wireframes

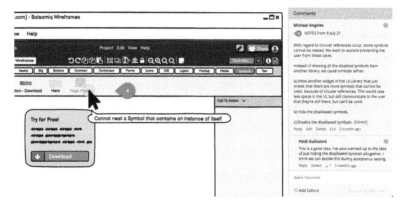

FIG 6.1: Notes with callouts can be added with wireframe comments, so there's no question about what the feedback refers to.

on their own time. We do this quite often with our team; being in different time zones can make real-time feedback a challenge, but not impossible. Some wireframing tools allow you to add callouts directly to areas of the design being critiqued (**FIG 6.1**).

In both real-time and asynchronous review sessions, we take notes directly in our wireframing tool in a way that the whole team can see them. We mention or tag people by name to refer to the person who made an observation, so they can verify that we got their comment right and follow up, in case there were aspects that they hadn't finished processing. This allows the team to follow what we logged and it helps the designer to correlate the changes discussed with the relevant parts of the interface.

Keep it focused

Sometimes it's hard to keep the discussion focused on analysis and critical thinking. The best thing you can do is to model good feedback and reset the discussion when it goes off the rails.

You'll need to learn to discern the difference between feedback that can further your cause and reactions or commentary that isn't useful. You want to elicit observations that always return to the question, "Does this help the user reach their goals?" At this point you may feel invested in specific design directions, but your job is to advocate for the user, not for the design.

This is not an us vs. them situation. In a sense, you're acting as a mediator between the design in its current state and the product team—of which you are a part. You're all working as a whole to improve the product.

If you come to the conclusion in any of the discussions that the design doesn't help accomplish objectives—that's okay! This is why you take the time for critique. The analysis should help you determine why, so that you can go back and iterate on the idea.

Participating in a critique with others, and being able to detach yourself from your work are things that takes practice. Just remember that this process will lead you to produce a better product for your user. If you're able to improve your design as a result of critique—even if your colleagues repeatedly took it apart—then you can feel proud of your work. Remember: *you are not your design*.

End the session by thanking your participants and setting expectations for what will happen next. Let them know that you will follow up with a summary of feedback and decisions for the next round of iteration.

ACTING ON FEEDBACK

In our design critiques, we usually summarize our notes in a project management app, then share the summary with the team. In your summary, describe what you reviewed and who participated.

You may also find it helpful to move the feedback into a spreadsheet. List each salient observation or comment, along with who offered it, so you can verify or clarify as needed. Add a column for the status of each feedback item to indicate whether the feedback will or will not be pursued. In *Presenting Design Work* (https://bkaprt.com/wfe45/06-05), Donna Spencer divides feedback into five categories, which you can use to mark feedback status:

- **Agree and now:** *The team agrees with the feedback and can implement it immediately.*
- **Agree and later:** *The team agrees with the feedback, but will need to implement it at a later time.*
- **Needs research:** *There isn't enough information to make a decision and further research, discussion, or analysis is required.*
- **Clarify:** *The team doesn't understand the feedback and needs to get clarification (this can occur more often when feedback sessions are conducted asynchronously).*
- **No:** *The team will not implement the feedback.*

After you share the summary and spreadsheet with your team, give people time to respond and clarify, or add to the feedback if necessary, based on these categories.

When there are no more remaining open issues, build a list of ways to improve the design. As you review the observations, organize them by screen or function in whatever way that will help you approach your next pass at the wireframe.

If the feedback revealed straightforward changes, you might be able to tackle them quickly: take the solutions and synthesize them into the design.

If the feedback found that the design left out important information, or made the wrong assumptions about particular use cases, you'll need to spend more time reviewing research, exploring solutions, and adding detail to your wireframes. For example, perhaps you learned that the wireframes for a signup process failed to consider what happens if the user doesn't receive the necessary verification email. You might need to do a technical review first to learn about the available options before updating the wireframes.

When you update your wireframes based on feedback, you can show the original wireframe and feedback, alongside an updated version, to your reviewers for discussion or approval (**FIG 6.2**).

Whatever the critique revealed, remember that your goal with feedback is to gauge effectiveness and make improvements with the project goals in mind. Circle back to the problem statement when you consider proposals for new ideas. Ask

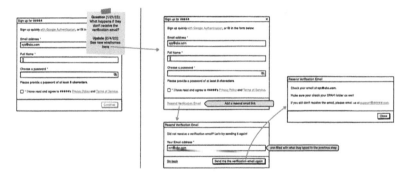

FIG 6.2: You can show old and new wireframes side-by-side to make it easier for reviewers to see what changed.

yourself if the new direction satisfies user needs and goals, and make sure that you didn't just add things based on the whims of others. Design by committee is rarely successful.

FEEDBACK IS A CYCLE

Once you've integrated everyone's feedback and created some new and improved wireframes, it's time to get ready to start the critique process again. Giving and receiving feedback as part of the design process is one of the best ways to collaborate on a product team.

You should be able to use this feedback process with larger, most established teams as well as on smaller, scrappier teams. Having a structured framework for critique will enable your team to give useful feedback that can be translated into improved wireframes.

Providing regular feedback during wireframe phases leads to shipping products that effectively meet their objectives. Incorporating well-managed and thoughtful feedback reduces risk and guides iterations towards better solutions. And, if you've made it this far, there's a great chance that your team will deliver a highly desirable and usable product. You're almost there!

CROSSING THE FINISH LINE

Design isn't finished until somebody is using it.
—**BRENDA LAUREL** (https://bkaprt.com/wfe45/07-01)

AT THIS POINT, YOUR IDEA has passed through enough check-points and you're preparing to launch it into the world. Don't be surprised if a lot more people start showing interest now. To people outside of the product triad, your work may not feel real or relevant until coding begins. Executives, quality assurance, marketing, sales, support, clients, and others will all want to start reviewing, discussing, and planning. Brace yourself!

There are three critical phases that your wireframe designs should go through before you officially call them done: presenting them to a larger audience, handing off to code, and following through after the product's release. Let's look at each phase more closely.

PRESENTING YOUR WIREFRAMES

Presenting your designs to a broader audience can help other teams understand what's coming and how it may affect them down the road. Or, it might serve as a "pitch" to your clients or executives to get sign-off or approval. Use this time to build a shared understanding of the project and to create a plan for it moving forward.

Start by establishing context

When you begin your presentation, take a moment to explain what everyone is looking at. People might not be expecting wireframes. Th core of a wireframe is structure, so be sure to tell your audience that you're making an intentional choice to show structure over style at this point in the project—and show how you can focus on solving the problems users may encounter without being distracted by imagery, branding, and colors.

Mention that you're using wireframes because they are quick to make and easy to revise. This may encourage others to offer feedback they might otherwise hold back. What matters most is the quality of the final product, so getting input even this late in the game will allow you to fix any oversights. Better to learn about them now than after the product ships.

You might start by showing the very early wireframes that set the stage for the project, to showcase how they evolved from problem statement to structural outline, to multiple high-level concepts. Jumping straight to the proposed design can be jarring to someone who might be seeing it for the first time. Seeing its origins builds credibility because it shows that you were thoughtful and diligent.

Presenting wireframes allows the audience to focus on how users will flow through the product and content. A highly polished visual design could give the appearance of a final design that's ready for production, but at this point you'd rather build consensus around a solution—one that everyone can rally around by surfacing pain points and showing how those can impact business metrics.

Tell your design story

Regardless of who you're presenting to, telling a good story is an effective way to capture your audience's attention and show them what your new concept can do for users and for the business. A great story can captivate your audience and build empathy. It can also help put the audience in the right frame of mind when they encounter new or unexpected ideas.

Craft your presentation like a story with a beginning, middle, and end. Try this structure for your presentation:

- **Start with the project background.** Something led to the need for the wireframes you're presenting—a previous version that missed the mark, an existing tool that required an update, or a new feature that needed integration. Start with a clear statement about the project's purpose and what work has been done to date.
- **Introduce the user(s) whose problems you intend to solve.** If you have personas, you can use them here. Clearly state their problem and why they need something easier to use. Referring to a specific persona or use case will allow everyone to empathize with them and see the concept from their perspective. This is a great device to use throughout the presentation and during the rest of the design process. It shows that you made decisions based on real users and not just your opinion.
- **Demonstrate how the design works from the user's perspective.** Walk through common tasks the user would need to perform to reach their goals and explain the improvements you made. This will show the concept's value in a real-world scenario and how the business will benefit.

You don't need to walk your audience through every single step you took and every option you tried—you'll lose their attention. Instead, try to make your presentation compelling and interesting, showing only the most relevant steps and decision points along the way.

Telling the story of your wireframes should help you to communicate all the work you put into understanding the totality of the project. Articulate what affects users, how that affects the business, and the best paths to a solution at this time. If you can get the decision makers to understand these different points, they'll help make the project a reality.

Build trust

It's important that the entire group understands all the steps you took and all the reasons behind each decision. Briefly covering each phase of design will build trust as the project moves forward.

It's important to build trust in this process, not just for this project, but for the projects that will follow. To do this well, consider the perspectives of each of the main voices in the room when you prepare your presentation, including concerns such as the time and resources you needed to build the product, the impact to the support and documentation team, and the effect of this design on sales and customers. Acknowledging your stakeholders' concerns when presenting your wireframes will help them feel heard and included in the process.

You also build trust through honesty and transparency. Here are a few tips to demonstrate transparency during a presentation:

- **Admit uncertainty.** Being humble helps get the audience on your side. You may be presenting to subject matter experts, and if you come off as having all the answers, you could appear dismissive. By mentioning areas of your wireframe that you're unsure about or have open questions about, you can build a more collaborative atmosphere. Incorporating another person's ideas can get them more invested in the design and turn them into an advocate. This is helpful when you have a room full of decision makers who can be an ally for the project moving forward.
- **Prepare alternative options.** If there are parts of your design that you suspect might face resistance, have some alternative options ready. It's better to show that you've considered many possible outcomes than to let people think that you knew something was possibly missing and dismissed it. If you've taken the time to explore many ideas, you should have a few backup ideas ready to go. Perhaps you have some ideas that you know are easier to implement but might be a bit less ideal for users. Keep those in your back pocket just in case.

- **Address challenges.** Don't shy away from mentioning issues that may negatively affect teams or could make their lives temporarily difficult, such as technical debt that could be incurred or deadlines that might slip. Being honest about both the positives and negatives will increase your trustworthiness and build goodwill with teams going forward.

If you can show that you've followed a deliberate process to get to this point, it should be easier to be open about any remaining challenges, unknowns, or variables. Being open will invite your audience to participate in the solutions and act as a partner rather than a checkpoint.

Listen and share

You've made it through your presentation, and now it's time to open the floor for questions and feedback. Listen (just like we recommended for design critiques). Don't feel the need to immediately defend any decisions. Instead, work to fully understand what the person is saying and where they're coming from. Feeling unheard and ignored can damage goodwill.

When the meeting is nearly concluded, recap everything you discussed. List any decisions made, address any questions, and reiterate what steps will be taken for each. Clear communication about what comes next is very important for the future of the project and for the collaboration that's needed to turn it into a real product.

Finally: Congratulations! Getting to the point where you're able to present your work is a huge accomplishment. If you've spent the necessary time to craft a thorough presentation, that means you've done a good job. You should have a clear set of next steps to tackle, as well as the support from everyone involved in the project.

COMPLETING THE HANDOFF
TO PRODUCTION CODE

Think back to our story from Chapter 5 about how one of our first UX teams created "perfect" designs that the developers mostly ignored.

Yeah, we're trying to avoid that.

Ideally, you've used the wireframing process as a tool for communication. You've made sure everyone on the team knows what you're building and why. When people in product, design, and development roles are all on the same page, translating wireframes to code should be a straightforward process with few hiccups.

Continuous and organized communication helps alleviate implementation problems before they happen. Aside from taking time to talk through the wireframes together, here are a few techniques you can use to ensure a smooth handoff to developers.

Create frontend prototypes

Wireframes are meant to capture and represent the frontend (user-facing layer), so working prototypes can often be coded quickly, especially if they're based on an existing framework or templates. To be clear, we're talking about writing code in the same language as the real product, not using a prototyping tool.

If you're not a developer, ask a colleague to code a rough (or polished, depending on their bandwidth) sample of the wireframed frontend, so you can share it with team members and stakeholders.

These prototypes are a perfect example of an effective hand-off artifact that can align team members. They also might reveal technical challenges or design issues before you've committed any real time to writing production code.

Stay in communication

As the product is being developed, new errors or stress cases might arise. Advocate for communication lines to stay open during development so you can iterate quickly on design solutions.

You can do this proactively by going through the wireframes together with the dev team. That's what product designer Jenny Wen recommends in "How to Work Effectively With Engineers":

> *Instead of leaving tickets or Slack-ing back and forth about polish, save time by combing through the experience together. You can be precise about the implementation feedback you give and work through any design details together. (https://bkaprt. com/wfe45/07-02)*

Even solutions that don't require a long time to design can slow down the process. Try to include a little room in your schedule to deal with last-minute changes and issues.

Plan for changes as a team

Don't let your involvement stop once coding starts. Make sure that everyone understands your wireframes and that they translate easily to code. Be present for the initial phases of interface development to see how the wireframes match up with the frontend code. Once you've done this a few times, you can create a library of wireframe controls that have known counterparts with live code components.

Be prepared for things to change, even at the last minute. Priorities change, business goals shift, stakeholders are fickle. Real life is messy and humans aren't robots (thank goodness). Some things will always be outside of your control, but don't lose hope. Set your sights on the next release cycle and look for every opportunity to communicate and collaborate.

FOLLOWING THROUGH

When you've put in so much time and effort to turn user problems into product solutions, it can be hard to grasp that the work is just now starting for many other people in your company. Tasks in marketing, support, analytics, testing, and documentation are all kicked off with a working product. Even the product manager role reboots once the new work reaches customers and they start to provide feedback and requests.

The best thing you can do to conclude your design work is to connect with the people whose work starts now. Think of them as your extended team. Help them understand your design decisions and the thinking behind them, and, in turn, learn what they need from you and how you might be able to make their jobs easier. You might even learn how to get them involved in the design process earlier next time.

Track post-release feedback

Some companies engage actively with their community to understand how users work with their products and to solicit feedback for new and existing features. These tasks often fall to user researchers, but you can do this even without a dedicated research team.

There was a time when our company was so small and scrappy that many of our designers had to pitch in to do customer support. This isn'tt ideal for everyone, but for us it provided interesting opportunities to hear first-hand reactions to new ideas, and even test new features with select groups of users. Occasionally, we'd even preview wireframes with customers before a feature was implemented.

If you can't be on the ground floor of customer support yourself, your support team might be able to keep track of customer requests in your user forums and support tickets. If they're tracking and categorizing this information, they should be able to give you a sense of the frequency and severity of users' reported challenges. We use an internal tool that shows the number of feature issues and bugs at a glance, somewhat like a dashboard (**FIG 7.1**).

FIG 7.1: We created this issue tracker dashboard to monitor community feedback and requests over time.

If your support team has an issue tracker or log, find out if you can get access to it as well, or if they can send you regular reports.

Learn as you go

Once you've concluded your wireframing work, take some time to reflect on the project. It's likely that something (or multiple things) happened that you didn't want or agree with. There might have been delays, misunderstandings, or wrong turns.

To pinpoint the cause of these challenges, ask yourself:

1. Did the problem occur during one of the phases? For example, were the product requirements incorrect? Did the design not match the stated problem? Was the code buggy?

2. Did the problem occur during a handoff? Was it the result of a misunderstanding, misplaced expectations, or poor communication?

Most of the time, the bigger problems will arise from the second instance—from people (including you) *thinking* that they understand something when they really don't. Imperfect execution *within* phases will usually yield a good enough result for most of your customers. But communication problems *between* phases can really make a product suffer.

Miscommunication requires multiple people, and real people are imperfect. Yet we often choose to ignore this reality when it comes to project communication.

Instead of pointing fingers at your teammates' behavior, ask yourself what you could have done differently to account for their unique traits. Having a team-oriented mindset means assuming responsibility for what ships, regardless of your role or contribution. It also means that instead of blaming individuals, it's better to assume everyone is trying to do their best and looking for ways to improve the process.

As you start to think about what you could have done differently, or what you'd like to do differently next time, reflect on the effort you put into the project and how you might have allocated it better:

- What levers at your disposal can you move to improve the process?
- How might you adapt the process to better leverage your teammates' strengths?
- How can you provide support during handoff to improve communication and understanding?
- How can you influence people through leading by example or promoting a team-oriented mindset?

So, when—not *if*—things don't go as expected, take the opportunity to learn where communication and expectations broke down, and work on strengthening those points. The success of any project hinges on the people involved and their ability to work together to produce something better than what they could have accomplished separately. That means building strong relationships with everyone involved. Wireframes can greatly facilitate communication and collaboration, but only when people are ready to work together.

WIREFRAMING IS A MINDSET

When we look at what makes wireframes valuable to product design, the output they generate isn't what stands out. Their value comes from the process of wireframing—how it helps teams iterate, explore, and refine their design ideas, and how it keeps teams aligned and communicating throughout the process.

Learning to create effective wireframes requires a paradigm shift toward seeing them as a flexible, creative tool, rather than as a means to an end. Wireframes should perform multiple functions and go through distinct phases—from aiding in visualizing the problem and building connections, to designing high-level flows, content relationships, and critical interactions—all while remaining open to feedback and change.

When we think of wireframes as a tool for thinking and communicating, the audience for wireframes and their uses become much broader. Don't restrict yourself to using them only with the people who make the product. Everyone benefits when their expectations align and they're able to participate in product conversations. Bringing people together is wireframing's superpower.

ACKNOWLEDGMENTS

THANK YOU, DESIGNERS AND PRODUCT people for generously sharing how you work. The spirit of openness and inclusivity in the product design community is what allows us to continue writing about making products. To Christina Wodtke and Louis Rosenfeld in particular, thank you for showing me how to turn obsessive organization into a UI design career.

I'm grateful to Adam Connor, Donna Spencer, and Victor Lombardi for providing feedback early in the process. To Sharina Wunderink, Lisa Maria Marquis, Katel LeDû, and everyone at ABA, thank you for helping us transform our ideas into a compelling story. Peldi Guilizzoni, thanks for trusting me to contribute to the creation of a wireframing product aimed at solving the right problems. To the UX education duo of Billy and Leon—I'm proud of what we can accomplish as a team!

Last, to Ali—thank you for your patience and encouragement as I mused and processed my way through writing this book.

—**Michael Angeles**

To Katel LeDû, Lisa Maria Marquis, Leslie Zaikis, Sharina Wunderink, and the amazing team at A Book Apart: you made this book immeasurably better and were a dream to work with. You all are something special!

To all the Balsamici: you've been such a great family for the past ten years. To Peldi Guilizzoni: thanks for supporting this project and giving us your trust. To Billy Carlson and Michael Angeles: I couldn't have asked for better coauthors; we made a great team. To Francesca Fabbri: working with you is effortless; thanks for your consistent support and encouragement.

To all the caring, hard-working folks on software teams stretching outside of their job descriptions because there's no one else to do it: your work may go unrecognized, but it is not unnoticed. You do much more for usability than you realize.

To the UX pioneers and practitioners who came before me and to those who will come after: thanks for pushing UX forward and championing human-centered design.

—**Leon Barnard**

This book would not be possible if it weren't for our incredible team at Balsamiq. Thank you to Peldi Guilizzoni for the inspiration to write a book, and for fostering such a wonderful, creative, and experimental environment to work and thrive in. To my coauthors Michael and Leon, you are a dream to collaborate with. This book is better because we worked together, as any good design team should.

To the wonderful team at A Book Apart, who took a few passionate designers and turned them into writers. We've learned so much from you, and this book was brought to life with your tireless work. Sincerest gratitude to Katel, Lisa Maria, and Sharina.

To my family. My parents have always been incredibly supportive of my creativity and—look at me, I cowrote a book! To my loving wife Michelle, and my incredible kids, Will, Annie, Coco, and Gigi. I love you to the moon and back.

My deepest appreciation to all the incredible folks in the design community. I am a professional designer because countless folks throughout my career decided to help me in some way. Thank you.

—**Billy Carlson**

RESOURCES

Sketching and wireframing

- *Sketching User Experiences* by Bill Buxton. A great place to start from, to understand the context for wireframing. A huge inspiration for our book.
- Balsamiq Wireframing Academy. A bit of self-promotion here! Contains articles and videos produced by us, and tons of great wireframing lessons and resources from a wide range of experts (https://bkaprt.com/wfe45/08-01).
- "Project Wireframes" Google Slides Template. This template is specifically designed for presenting wireframe projects (https://bkaprt.com/wfe45/08-02).

UI and visual design

- *Designing Interfaces: Patterns for Effective Interaction Design* by Jenifer Tidwell, Charles Brewer, and Aynne Valencia. A great handbook for UI patterns and practices—it makes UI design make sense.
- *100 Things Every Designer Needs to Know About People* by Susan Weinschenk. A fantastic primer on understanding how and why we behave the way we do when using digital products, based on behavioral science.
- *Web Form Design: Filling in the Blanks* by Luke Wroblewski. An oldie, but goodie. Everything you'll ever need to know about designing forms.
- *Atomic Design* by Brad Frost. A deeper exploration of the topic of controls, patterns, and templates that also dives into the implementation side of things.
- *Refactoring UI* by Adam Wathan and Steve Schoger. Makes UI design principles like color, spacing, and contrast easy to understand and apply.
- *Ordering Disorder: Grid Principles for Interaction Design* by Khoi Vinh. A great read if you really want to understand why and how grids work so effectively for web layouts.

- Design challenge generators for practicing and refreshing your UI design skills:
- Sharpen (https://bkaprt.com/wfe45/08-03)
- Designercize (https://bkaprt.com/wfe45/08-04)
- Brief Up (https://bkaprt.com/wfe45/08-05)
- UpLabs Challenges (https://bkaprt.com/wfe45/08-06)

User experience

- *Practical UX Design* by Scott Faranello. An underappreciated gem that gives you all the best bits without any fluff.
- *101 Random UX Tips: Practical Bits for Novices and Experts* by William Ntim. Full of wisdom about designing better and working better as a designer.
- *Just Enough Research* by Erika Hall. A guidebook for using research to reduce risk and work on the right problem. Introduces the research process and different types of studies that can be utilized by product teams of any size or budget.
- *User Friendly: How the Hidden Rules of Design Are Changing the Way We Live, Work, and Play* by Cliff Kuang. Explains the origins of the field of user experience and walks through a wonderful series of examples of how listening to people makes better products, which makes happy customers.
- *Everyday Information Architecture* by Lisa Maria Marquis. Content organization is fundamental to UX. This book covers all the essentials of IA to help you plan before you design.
- *Don't Make Me Think* by Steve Krug. One of the first, and most effective books to bring usability awareness to a lay audience. A classic for good reason.
- UX and usability articles from Nielsen Norman Group. The gold standard for research and advice on UX best practices. Updated regularly (https://bkaprt.com/wfe45/08-07).

Software process

- *UX for Lean Startups* by Laura Klein. Shows how UX should be integrated as a process on a software team, not used just a skill set. A great resource for any PM or product owner.
- *The Lean Product Playbook: How to Innovate with Minimum Viable Products and Rapid Customer Feedback* by Dan Olsen. Another great book for product managers that shows how to maximize the effectiveness of your team and resources, and launch successful products.

Design and creativity

- *Presenting Design Work* by Donna Spencer. A brief, approachable book with tips for structuring and giving effective design presentations that lead to actionable feedback.
- *Discussing Design* by Adam Connor and Aaron Irizarry. A deep dive for those looking to incorporate structured design critique into their product design process.
- *Design is Storytelling* by Ellen Lupton. A playbook for how to use storytelling to communicate new ideas, propose new solutions, and help people understand new perspectives.
- *Creativity, Inc.* by Ed Catmull. An inside look at the creative process at Pixar that gives a sense of the herculean effort of turning ideas into feature animated films.
- "Creativity In Management" by John Cleese. The most entertaining talk you'll ever hear about creativity that also gets right at the heart of it (https://bkaprt.com/wfe45/08-08, video).
- "Immaculate Heart College Art Department Rules" by Corita Kent. A timeless set of rules for creatives working in the studio (https://bkaprt.com/wfe45/08-09).

REFERENCES

Shortened URLs are numbered sequentially; the related long URLs are listed below for reference.

Chapter 1

01 01   https://www.billbuxton.com/bookFlyer.pdf

01-02   https://www.penguinrandomhouse.com/books/216369/creativity-inc-by-ed-catmull-with-amy-wallace/

01-03   https://www.kcrw.com/culture/shows/good-food/noma-woks-of-life-remembering-sylvia-wu-carrots/rene-redzepi-best-restaurant-in-the-world-reinvention

01-04   https://www.oreilly.com/library/view/designing-interfaces-3rd/9781492051954/

Chapter 2

02-01   https://101randomuxtips.com/

02-02   https://uxdesign.cc/documenting-is-designing-how-documentation-drives-better-design-outcomes-3ebd87a33d57

02-03   https://abookapart.com/products/everyday-information-architecture

02-04   https://wireframestogo.com/9044-Wireflows/

02-05   https://www.oreilly.com/library/view/ux-for-lean/9781449335007

02-06   https://balsamiq.com/learn/articles/wireframes-content-modeling/

02-07   https://twitter.com/david_perell/status/1373025352247873538

02-08   https://parahumans.wordpress.com/2012/07/24/interlude-12/

02-09   https://sharpen.design/

02-10   https://tannerchristensen.com/blog/2019/6/17/design-edge-cases-and-where-to-find-them

02-11   https://www.producttalk.org/

Chapter 3

03-01   https://www.nngroup.com/videos/jakobs-law-internet-ux/

03-02   https://ui-patterns.com/

03-03   https://balsamiq.com/learn/courses/how-to-design-navigation/

Chapter 4

04-01 https://www.nngroup.com/articles/principles-visual-design/

Chapter 5

05-01 https://dan-olsen.com/

05-02 https://uxdesign.cc/design-annotations-that-will-make-your-developers-happy-d376d4453d9d

05-03 https://www.oreilly.com/library/view/97-things-every/9781492085164/

05-04 https://balsamiq.com/learn/videos/the-process-behind/content-first-design/

Chapter 6

06-01 https://www.creativelivesinprogress.com/article/corita-kent

06-02 https://www.oreilly.com/library/view/discussing-design/9781491902394/

06-03 https://gist.github.com/ezl/49f0f9d1c702e51ca96f9b0f67cf9400

06-04 https://abookapart.com/products/design-for-cognitive-bias

06-05 https://abookapart.com/products/presenting-design-work

Chapter 7

07-01 http://www.tauzero.com/Brenda_Laurel/

07-02 https://medium.com/dropbox-design/how-to-work-effectively-with-engineers-19afbcc9f326

Chapter 8

08-01 https://balsamiq.com/learn/

08-02 https://docs.google.com/presentation/u/0/?tgif=c&ftv=1

08-03 https://sharpen.design/

08-04 https://designercize.com/

08-05 https://briefup.co/

08-06 https://www.uplabs.com/challenges

08-07 https://www.nngroup.com/articles/

08-08 https://www.youtube.com/watch?v=Pb5olIPO62g

08-09 https://www.creativelivesinprogress.com/article/corita-kent

INDEX

ABOUT A BOOK APART

We cover the emerging and essential topics in web design and development with style, clarity, and above all, brevity—because working designer-developers can't afford to waste time.

COLOPHON

The text is set in FF Yoga and its companion, FF Yoga Sans, both by Xavier Dupré. Headlines and cover are set in Titling Gothic by David Berlow.

 This book was printed in the United States using FSC certified papers.

ABOUT THE AUTHORS

Michael Angeles has been an interface designer at Balsamiq since 2012. He has published articles and spoken at conferences on the topic of wireframing for product design. He created the IA Slash and Konigi blogs on interface design, and served as advisor and cofounder of the Information Architecture Institute.

Leon Barnard leads the education team at Balsamiq. He uses his extensive experience as a UX designer to teach user interface design basics and wireframing to an audience of mostly non-designers via the Balsamiq Wireframing Academy. He loves helping people and technology get along better together.

Billy Carlson is a design educator at Balsamiq, where he helps new and non-designers learn best practices for all phases of user interface and digital product design. He teaches university-level UX and design thinking courses, and, as a designer since 2005, he's worked on myriad products and led large UX teams at various organizations.

Printed in the USA
CPSIA information can be obtained
at www.ICGtesting.com
JSHW011621221023
50548JS00007B/28